SHADY JUSTICE

RENA KOONTZ

Shady Justice

Copyright © 2024 Rena Koontz

Editor: Tamara Eaton

This book is a work of fiction. The names, characters, places, and incidents are the products of the author's imagination or are used fictitiously. Any resemblance to actual events, business establishments, locales, or persons, living or dead, is entirely coincidental.

All rights reserved. No part of this book may be reproduced, stored in a retrieval system, or transmitted in any form or by any means (electronic, mechanical, photocopying, recording, or otherwise) without the prior written permission of both the copyright owner and the publisher. The only exception is brief quotations in printed reviews.

The scanning, uploading, and distribution of this book via the Internet or via any other means without the permission of the publisher is illegal and punishable by law. Please purchase only authorized electronic editions, and do not participate in or encourage electronic piracy of copyrighted materials.

Your support of the author's rights is appreciated.

Published in the United States of America by

Rena Koontz

2200 Kings Highway 3L

Suite 66

Port Charlotte, FL. 33980

renakoontz.com

❦ Formatted with Vellum

For my fellow news reporters

SHADY JUSTICE

1

The woman was so badly beaten, Steel Chaney vomited his breakfast bagel in the grass at the side of the concrete driveway. So much for bragging that after twenty years on the job, he'd seen it all.

Christ, there was nothing left of her face to identify. Her mouth was a bloody hollow where teeth should be. The tips of all ten fingers were scorched black. Were they burned before or after she died? For her sake, he hoped it was postmortem. Someone sure as hell didn't want her identified.

Chaney spit the last of the sour taste away, wiped his mouth on his coat sleeve, and turned back to the car. The poor woman was stuffed inside the trunk on her back, her legs pinned beneath her. They had to be broken. Blood soaked her clothes, seeping to the area rug underneath her body, turning it pitch black. Her killer had wrapped her in this piece of carpet to transport her from the murder site. Blood matted in her dirty blond hair where her skull was crushed. Caked strands knotted around gold circle earrings. Her eyes were swollen shut, a palette of eggplant purple and midnight blue. A bloodied gold chain fell toward the back of her neck. Robbery was not a motive for this act of violence.

He narrowed his focus to the interior of the trunk. Empty except for three forty-pound bags of cat litter shoved to the rear. What the fuck?

"Steel?"

He turned toward Parker Bentley, the rookie detective he mentored. As rookies go, she was smarter than most and still hungry to learn. He'd balked at taking on a trainee, assuming his seniority exempted him from babysitting. It hadn't. His argument, that a three-month mentoring period was ridiculous given the years and experience most cops already had by the time they expressed interest in the detective bureau, fell on deaf ears, all because two years ago the mayor got his tit in the wringer over some detective new to the job who went rogue and then claimed lack of training. So now, they had training.

He'd checked out Parker Bentley, looking for any excuse to dump a woman hoping to do a man's job. She'd been a terror practically from her first day as a boot, coming up through the ranks in uniform with honors and accolades and an impressive arrest record. Those threatened by her, women and men alike, referred to her as Bitch Bentley. After knowing her awhile, he was certain it was said behind her back. He was even more confident she didn't give a damn.

Bentley shook his hand the first day they met. "I'm not interested in fetching your coffee or fucking you. You're supposed to be the best. I already know the criminal code. What I want from you is every bit of knowledge you have regarding detective work that I can't learn from a manual. I don't give a shit about your love life, your prostate or your wet dreams. In return, I'll make you proud to have mentored me." So far, she had.

She held out a bottle of water. "You going soft on me?"

He smiled. "Maybe. Knew we had a body. Shouldn't have

eaten on the way." His mouth welcomed the cool water. "Any idea who she is?"

"Not yet. No license plate. If this is her car, she's a better woman than I."

"What do you mean?"

"The car is clean inside. I mean immaculate. Not a tissue or an umbrella or a crumbled store receipt under the seat. The trunk where she ended up dead is spotless. Not even a snow scraper left in there from winter. No woman I know keeps a car this clean."

He snickered. "You going sexist on me?"

"No, I'm being honest. A woman's car is like her purse. Anything we might need is in there. If this is her vehicle, she wasn't human."

He loved her sense of humor, even in the face of murder.

He took another swig. "So, car owner unknown for now. What else?"

"Not much. Thank goodness it's cool this morning. I don't think decomposition is an issue."

A polite way of saying the body was fresh. The temperature had dropped last night to the fifties. Fall was trying to overtake summer, but slowly here in the City of Pittsburgh. Today it would be eighty degrees again. They stepped closer to the trunk. No handbag visible unless it was under the body. He should be so lucky to find her wallet and ID. A blood-stained ten-dollar bill peeked out of her ripped blouse as if jammed between her breasts. "Maybe she was a hooker."

Bentley rolled her eyes "An entire crime scene and you focus on her breasts. I have a caveman for a partner."

He was, to some extent. Bentley was dragging him kicking and screaming into the twenty-first century where women were equals. He stood with one foot in the good old days, when he didn't have to admit women like Bentley were superior to him. Didn't mean he didn't respect the hell out of her and women in general. He'd take a bullet for Bentley. Few people he'd say that about, including his two ex-wives.

"I saw the money. Always a motive for murder." One side of Bentley's mouth lifted in a smirk. She wasn't buying it. "Who called it in?"

She pointed toward a young man leaning against his garage door wiping snot from his nose with his sleeve, barefoot, the front of his pants wet. Yeah, finding a dead woman in your driveway would make anyone piss their pants.

"That gentleman, and I use the term loosely." Bentley consulted her mini-iPad. He still preferred pencil and notebook, but she was all about electronics. "Says his name is Dickey Sharpei. Like the dog. Lives here with his parents and sister. Claims he doesn't know the woman, doesn't recognize the car, doesn't know anything about anything. I didn't have a chance to run his name yet to see if he has a record. This is a top-notch neighborhood and, if you ask me, he looks out of place."

Chaney's eyes darted up and down the asphalt street. This community was an upscale suburb just outside the city. Two-story houses with shiny, power-washed aluminum siding, colorful window boxes in full bloom at the end of summer, and manicured lawns. Perennials decorated the paths up to the front doors and varied door wreaths and welcome signs greeted a visitor. The weedy Sharpei landscaping around the single-family lot was less pristine than the neighbors, the siding on the house marred in spots and dirty all over, and not a blooming flower in sight. The entire property appeared slightly sullied compared to the other homes on the street. Likewise, Mr. Sharpei looked marginally below the decency bar in his tattered shorts, his uncut hair, and his dirty fingernails. Plus, he had the shakes. Nerves or did he need a hit of his drug of choice?

"You'll find a criminal history for sure. His face is familiar."

The names didn't always stick, but Chaney recognized him as one of the hundreds of druggies he'd arrested during his stint on the force. Drug possession and grand theft auto, he was certain. How much did the little snot have to do with this woman's murder?

"Who was first on the scene?"

"Unit six-seven over there. Sergeant Wayne Cubb is writing up a report for us now."

"Okay, tell me what you know as fact and what you think in theory." This was how he mentored her, never showing or lecturing, always expecting her to apply her knowledge to sort through the minutia of a crime. She was intelligent, book smart and street wise, and often saw what he didn't.

Bentley filled her lungs and used a stylus to scroll her screen. She printed in tiny block letters, unreadable for his aging eyeballs. He blamed it on the light reflecting off the iPad.

"Call came in at five forty-seven this morning. Dickey Sharpei over there reported an unknown car parked in his driveway. Claims he didn't touch anything, just saw the car and called the police. Says he doesn't recognize the vehicle. He didn't pop the trunk, Sergeant Cubb did. The car was locked but Cubb found the key fob balanced on top of the left front tire."

Sure, that's where every bad guy leaves the key. Chaney nodded.

"Those are facts that I find odd. Normal curiosity would make me look inside the car first for a clue as to who it belonged to if I didn't already know. Would I look in the trunk? Yeah, but maybe I'm unusually nebby."

A dozen years in this city and he still didn't understand Pittsburghese. "Unusually what? Your Pittsburgh accent is surfacing again."

Bentley blushed. She looked good with color on her face. "Sorry. It means nosy."

Chaney agreed. He'd be nebby too.

Bentley swiped at her screen. "Back to the facts. Sharpei says he was out partying last night. Says he was drunk as a skunk when he rolled home. That's a self-portrait. He thinks it was before three." She made air quotes around the word think. "Says there was no car here when a buddy dropped him off. He's having trouble remembering who brought him home. Imagine that. Claims he was intensely wasted. Again, his words. He stressed his intoxicated state more than once. Judging by the wrinkles, he slept in his clothes so maybe." Her shoulders moved up and down. "Never heard a thing until his phone rang this morning about five-thirty."

"Who woke him up?"

Bentley shrugged again. "He says it was a hang up. He took a piss, looked out his bedroom window and saw the car."

"And he immediately called the police? Why?"

"Exactly. The little shit is lying. That's theory. Sergeant Cubb found nothing in the glove box except the owner's manual. A small tin of opened breath mints was on the ground, under the driver's side." She held up a quart-sized plastic evidence bag. "Cubb bagged it so it didn't get kicked around. I was close to Mr. Sharpei. The breath mints aren't his. Sergeant Cubb asked Sharpei for permission to open the trunk, just to follow procedure.

"Sharpei denied recognizing the car or the woman. Cubb said the kid almost passed out when the trunk lid lifted. And he pissed himself."

She smiled at that. Bentley had a knack for discovering a person's weakness. She often used it against them.

"Cubb says Sharpei was adamant the car wasn't his and he didn't know the owner. While he was waiting for us, he called in the VIN number but the identification system is experiencing technical difficulties this morning."

She answered before he asked. "The automatic backup

went into meltdown last night and now VINNY is clogged trying to catch up. I put a rush on an ID."

Chaney studied their witness, then let his gaze roam across the house. "Anyone else at home?"

"No. Parents are away on a trip. Dickey doesn't remember where or when they return. He said maybe today, maybe next week. Said he thought it was a cruise. He said he has a sister but has no idea where she is."

"I wonder if everyone is away by coincidence."

Bentley frowned. "You don't believe in coincidence. Me either. That's all the facts. Here's what I think. Ole Dickey knows more than he says. Who finds a car in their driveway and doesn't look inside? We should bring him in for a heart to heart. I haven't touched the body yet but she's newly divorced, judging by the indentation on her ring finger. Or she was cheating. The autopsy will confirm it, but I don't think she's a natural blond. She needs a root job."

"How can you tell with all that blood?"

"Leaned all the way in with my flashlight. There's gray at her nape. I'm guessing she's middle aged. Anyone can wear tight jeans and a silky blouse but her hands look old. The skin on her neck isn't tight. That shoe peeking out from under her hip isn't what a young woman would wear."

"Maybe she has bad feet." His own shoes were pinching today.

"Always a possibility. My bet is this isn't her car. If it comes back hers, I'd be surprised. It's too damn clean. Possibly stolen. Might as well dump a body and a car all at once, right? But why in Sharpei's driveway? He's a two-bit nothing. What's he supposed to do with it?"

She absently scraped the cuticle on her thumb with her index finger, a nervous habit he'd learned meant she was uncomfortable with a situation. She rarely knew she did it. He'd seen her scratch it until it bled.

"This was a violent act, Steel, not a random carjacking gone bad. Her murder was calculated. I want a good look at her hands. Look at her fingernails, or what's left of them. She fought for her life. Some bastard is walking around with scratches on his arms and maybe his face." She scanned the techs surrounding the car. "I wish these folks would hurry up."

Bentley hated waiting.

They couldn't touch anything until the forensic team finished processing the scene. And they'd been notified an assistant district attorney was en route. Had to be Laquisha Moore, not his favorite. She was the only one who showed up at the location of a crime, acting like she was the detective. It was overstepping, in his mind. She risked contaminating his crime scene.

A forensic photographer already was clicking hundreds of pictures from every angle imaginable, even the underside of the car. Other forensic techs began a grid search of the area looking for evidence. No one commits a crime without leaving some type of forensic evidence behind, a fingerprint, a strand of hair or maybe clothing fibers. The trick would be finding that evidence and then matching it to their murderer.

Bentley watched the techs, wrinkling her nose at the cigarette butts that peppered the front lawn. The techs would collect each one, even though identifying them to the killer would be the proverbial needle in a haystack. The evidence pertaining to this woman's murder wasn't here.

"Why do you assume it's a man?"

Her lips pursed. "It doesn't feel female. That's theory. Too hard to cram this body in here. Our victim isn't a small woman. I guess one-hundred and sixty pounds or close to. That's dead weight and a lot to wrangle with. I could do it, but I train for that.

"Also, a woman plans better." Her hand swept the scene. "She wouldn't simply dump a car and a body in a driveway where anyone could see and hope it disappears. Everyone has camera doorbells these days. This was not the plan. Something changed."

"Maybe it wasn't planned. Could have been spontaneous, an act of passion. Maybe the killer wanted her found." He could see Bentley's mind at work.

"Found but not identifiable? Doesn't make sense. Spontaneous doesn't take the time to remove fingerprints. This is a bold statement, like fuck you. Also, not a woman's style."

Bentley pointed inside. "And this money. Some kind of insult tossed at her after she was stuffed in here. Maybe she was still conscious and could hear whatever words accompanied rough hands cramming it into her bra. Someone not only wanted to kill her, they wanted the last humiliating word."

A homicide was a puzzle and Bentley was good at putting the pieces together. She did make him proud. "Nice, Parker, real nice. I think it was a man, too. Let's talk to our witness."

They walked toward Sharpei. The kid was smoking like a charcoal grill, still crying.

"Long time no see, Sharpei." Steel flashed his badge. "Remember me?"

"I didn't have nothin' to do with this, Detective."

"With what?"

"With that woman."

"Who is she?"

"I don't know, I swear. I never seen her before."

"How'd she end up in your driveway, Dickey?"

"I don't know." He whined like a seven-year-old. "Honest, I don't."

"What about the car?"

"I never seen it before."

"Do you know who owns it?"

"No, no sir."

"You don't find it odd that a random car with a dead woman in the trunk winds up parked in your driveway?"

"I swear I don't know nothin' about it."

"C'mon, Dickey, I don't buy it. You told my partner you were partying last night. Did you come home with this woman and things got a little out of hand? Maybe she didn't want to continue the party and you lost your temper. Or—"

"No, no, I swear to you. I never saw her before or her ride."

"So, the car belongs to her?"

"I-I don't know, man. I'm just sayin' I don't know nothin' about this."

"How about if we go inside? Can we take a look around your house, Dickey? Maybe the lady's purse or jacket is inside."

"It ain't."

"Can we see for ourselves?"

"No, my parents ain't home. They don't like strangers in the house." He started to sob.

Steel laid his hand on his shoulder. "Okay, buddy, okay. How about if one of these officers accompanies you inside and you change your clothes? Let's discuss this further downtown. You'll think more clearly when you're not looking at a dead woman in your front yard. Maybe you'll have a change of heart and tell us the truth."

"Are you arresting me? Do I need a lawyer?"

The right corner of Bentley's mouth edged upward. Chaney chuckled.

"Do you need a lawyer?" she asked. "Only guilty people ask for their attorney. What'd you do to require legal consultation?"

"Nothin,' ma'am, I din't do nothin', honest. But I ain't talkin' no more without a lawyer."

Chaney motioned for a patrolman. Dammit. They wouldn't be able to interrogate him without his attorney present.

"All right, all right, we'll cross that bridge when we come to it." He nodded to the officer. "Escort Mr. Sharpei into his house to find a pair of shoes and clean pants. Make sure he has his cell phone so he can call his attorney once you're at the station. Before you make that call, Dickey, think about whether or not you want to stick to this story."

"It ain't a story, man, it's the truth. I don't know nothin' about her. This was supposed to be a joke."

"So, you do know something about it?"

"I don't detective, honest."

Chaney spotted the deputy coroner approaching the vehicle. "Take this piece of shit downtown. We'll deal with him later."

He nudged Bentley back toward the car. "A dead woman in the trunk of a car is a joke? Please explain the humor in that."

2

She'd been dead at least four hours, according to the deputy coroner's preliminary examination.

Chaney calculated the possibilities. She likely died around midnight or shortly after. It opened a four-to-five-hour window for the killer to deposit the car in the Sharpei driveway and Dickey claimed he arrived home around three. That narrowed the gap to two hours if he was telling the truth.

She'd been dumped before sunrise. Doorbell cameras might not be much help, but uniformed officers were canvassing the street and requesting the homeowners review their footage.

Bentley shadowed the coroner's movements, speaking softly into a key chain recorder. She liked to record procedural stuff and transcribe it at the office. It helped to hear her telling herself the facts, she said, like a second look. She was careful not to add personal commentary, particularly about the victim, in case the recording ended up in trial as discovery evidence, but she'd include every detail, right down to dandruff on one deputy coroner's shoulders in one case. Once, she remarked on his bad breath. Chaney had laughed and then gagged seeing her nose wrinkle as she typed her report. Maybe she was onto something with her system. She was a good investigator.

She came to stand beside him when the assistant district attorney arrived and peered into the rear of the car, then conferred with the forensic investigator and watched while the body was extricated from the trunk.

Laquisha Moore believed every murder site had an energy that clung to it, and she liked to see, smell, and feel it before she presented the court case to a jury. She'd never lost a criminal trial but Chaney didn't like her traipsing around, polluting his crime scene. Unlike him, she hadn't tossed her cookies at the sight of the dead woman. But she expected the detectives to work miracles and solve cases like the crime shows on television. There was no such thing as solving a murder in a one-hour prime time slot.

In court, she was a stunning barracuda in tailored suits, high heels, model-worthy makeup and long, lustrous hair. This morning she wore blue jeans and tennis shoes, her hair pulled tight in a knot on top of her head, her face bare. At least she didn't touch anything. She was a no-nonsense woman. He liked that part.

For that matter, so was Bentley, wearing little makeup at work and no jewelry, except for the tiny diamond studs in her ears. She could wow in heels and a cocktail dress, though. She'd been the topic of conversation at the Christmas party last year, all glittery eyes, FM heels, and a dress split up to her who-haw.

Bentley interrupted that memory. "No handbag, no wallet underneath the body. So far, she's still Jane Doe. The coroner said he smelled alcohol. Maybe this is a horrific end to a bad date. I don't see her hooking up with Dickey, though. Could be a Freudian thing on his part, I guess.

"They finished processing the car's interior. I didn't find any clues inside, did you?"

He'd searched after her, knowing she would be thorough but checking anyway. A dead end. He threw her the lead. "What do we do next, Detective?"

She smiled at the title, admitting once to him after too many beers that it had been her dream since childhood to wear a gold detective's badge. He suspected there was an ominous reason behind that goal, but he hadn't probed.

"Check missing person reports, but I'll bet tomorrow's lunch no one has reported her missing. We can press Dickey a little more, even though he lawyered up. He might crack. Without an ID, we're sort of stalled unless the doorbell cameras give us a lead."

They were. Miss Moore wasn't happy with that news. Chaney let Bentley deal with her, since Moore thought every man was out to derail her career. At least that had been his impression, that she hated men. He'd idly wondered one time watching Bentley and Moore interact if they were lovers. Bentley had spewed her beer the night he asked that, assuring her she didn't care which way she swung. Nevertheless, Moore lost the chip on her shoulder speaking with Bentley.

His stomach growled. Since he'd emptied it in the grass, he craved a cup of coffee. As if reading his mind, the local crime reporter for the TV station he regularly watched stepped into his line of vision, two lidded coffee cups in her hands. She grinned, raised the cups in the air and lured him to the yellow crime scene tape cordoning off the area.

"Good morning, Detective. Black right? I brought one for Parker, too." Funny, he'd been dealing with her longer than Bentley, but she never called him by his first name. He wondered again about Bentley's affinity with women.

"Lois Lane, fancy seeing you here." He reached for the Dunkin' cup.

Rylee Lapiz grinned. "Heard it on the scanner. Was on my

way to City Hall for a budget meeting. Thought I'd swing by and hear you tell me you can't tell me anything."

Chaney genuinely laughed, always amused by her optimism. "I can't tell you anything."

"I figured. Doesn't hurt to ask, though. Can you at least tell me if it's male or female? That would give me enough to tweet for the morning news and might make my editor tell me to stay here. The City's in financial trouble. There's nothing new to report there."

"Since when do you cover politics?" She'd been the crime reporter for more than two years, to his knowledge. Always hustling, even though her news station was rated fourth in the market. In his opinion, her station was the best and most accurate, even when it came to forecasting the weather, which his arthritis did equally as well.

"Covering for the beat guy. He called in sick. I hoped you'd rescue me and give me a story."

He laughed, admitting to himself that he enjoyed talking with her as much as he did verbally sparring with Bentley. In general, he hated the news media but, as reporters went, Lapiz was fair, totally unimpressed with herself despite having accumulated numerous journalism awards. She'd proven she was interested in only the facts and not sensational headlines, like her competitors. And she'd earned his trust a year ago when details about a murder were communicated to him with her in earshot. He'd instructed her the information was off the record and she'd kept her word and not reported it until he consented. It wouldn't hurt to toss her a crumb.

"Female."

"Old or young? White or black."

He chuckled. "You said only one question."

"Technically I didn't but—" Her focus moved behind him and he turned to see Bentley approaching, tapping the side of her face with her forefinger. She reached for the cup Lapiz held out.

"Old or young?" She directed her question to Bentley.

Bentley blew into the coffee cup. "Too hard to tell. That's all you get for now."

"It helps, thanks." She began furiously typing on her phone with her thumbs. Chaney marveled at the speed. He pecked his messages with one finger, the victim of sausage thumbs.

"Since when did you become so friendly with the media?" he whispered as they headed toward their respective vehicles.

"I'm not friendly with them. She's different. I told you about running into her at that club, how she was drunk off her ass."

"You said you poured her into a ride and sent her home."

"Yeah, well, it was my ride. I ended up driving her home and practically carrying her to her apartment door. What a shithole she lives in. I made sure she was okay before I left. Didn't want her choking on her own vomit. But you know how drunks like to talk so we talked. I decided she's not the enemy."

He narrowed his eyes. "What is she?"

Bentley's brows knitted. "She's just a schmuck like us trying to do a job. It doesn't hurt to give her a lead occasionally. It helps her and us. That way she's not nagging. Plus, I owe her a favor."

He wanted to pursue the conversation, but ADA Moore flagged them down.

"Are you two leaving already?" Her tone was one of admonishment. He let Bentley respond.

"The scene will be secured, ma'am. While the patrol units are canvassing the neighborhood for camera footage, we thought we'd talk to the witness who discovered the body. He's on his way downtown. She wasn't killed here so it's not the crime scene. He may have more information. We're waiting on the vehicle registration records. The car will be towed to the crime lab, and we've requested a uniformed officer remain posted here for at least the next forty-eight hours. The homeowners don't seem to be in town. There's nothing more we can do at the moment but if you prefer we remain here, I will."

That's it, Bentley, throw it back on her. Rylee Lapiz stood at the property's edge, her ears perked.

"Identification is paramount. Without teeth or fingerprints, the car seems our only lead." Moore emphasized those words, as if he and Bentley didn't know that.

"Yes, ma'am, that and the witness."

Rylee's eyebrows shot to her hairline, and she typed furiously. What the hell, he wasn't disseminating the information. Besides, Bentley liked her. Oh, to be a fly on the wall when those two were drunk together. Bentley hadn't said she was inebriated but he knew she could throw back beers with the best of them.

Laquisha continued, "I also think—"

That was the last straw for him. "With all due respect, ma'am, I don't tell you how to prosecute your cases. We know how to process a crime scene and investigate a murder."

Laquisha glared at him with an expression designed to intimidate. It didn't.

"Very well. Please keep me apprised of whatever you learn." She dismissed them with a wave of her hand and stomped off. He turned to his partner.

"Breakfast first?" His stomach continued to remind him he was hungry.

"Sure. Ole Dickey can stew for a while."

3

Rylee Lapiz checked her vibrating phone as the finance chairman droned on and on about the city's financial woes. Half of these council members were up for re-election and didn't want to raise taxes, but he was telling them they had no choice.

She read the text from her friend, Tessa. **My mother didn't come home last night. She's such a slut.**

Since separating from her father, Tessa's mother had been drinking like a camel, and spending money like a billionaire. She wanted to bankrupt her soon-to-be ex-husband, destroy his good business name, and ruin him personally. Peter Owens had unsuccessfully sought election to city council, campaigning on his solid family life, his faith, and his record for giving back to the community. He was a popular car dealer who seemed to have his hands in every charitable cause. Too bad Pearl Owens caught him with his hands all over his secretary, his pants down and the woman bent over his antique oak desk. She wasn't his only discretion, either.

Despite Pearl's attempts to publicly humiliate Owens, he'd lost by only a small margin and vowed to run again, promising to bring his fiscal expertise to this economically struggling metropolis. He sat three rows in front of her in an expensive three-piece suit, an attractive, middle-aged man with salt and pepper hair. He took care of himself physically, running daily and posting his time and distance on his social media pages. Like anyone cared.

Tessa had kept her abreast of the escalating behind-the-scenes arguments between her parents, which in Rylee's opinion, made him a little less appealing. She'd witnessed some herself, peeking out of Tessa's upstairs bedroom door while the couple fought. Mrs. Owens was a woman scorned who swore she'd stop at nothing to destroy her husband of more than thirty years.

Rylee discreetly returned the text. **Covering City Council for Geno. Can't talk now. Drinks later?**

And Tessa's response, **Call me when you can.**

The meeting recessed for a morning break. Peter Owens smiled and extended his hand when he saw her. "Good morning, Rylee. You're always a bright spot in an otherwise gloomy room."

She'd been honest with her friend. Her father was a little creepy. She shook his hand, the hairs on the back of her neck pinching as he held it a little too long.

"I was disappointed I didn't see you at the rally last night. I'd hoped for some media coverage."

"Yes, sir. Politics isn't my beat. I'm certain someone was assigned to the event. I'm only here this morning to cover for a colleague who called in sick." She wiggled her hand out of his.

"Well after I'm elected, I'm going to speak to your bosses about assigning you to City Hall. I follow all your stories. You write and speak well and usually are right on the money. We could use some accurate reporting around here."

A tiny voice in her head whispered to hold her tongue. She didn't listen.

"Geno Georges has covered City Hall for years, Mr. Owens. He's won awards for his work. He's an excellent reporter."

He popped a breath mint in his mouth and offered one to her. His mouth spread into a wide grin, almost clown-like. "What's with the mister, sweetheart? You're my daughter's best friend. You're like a daughter to me. Call me Pete. I'm not criticizing your colleague, merely saying I'd rather have a reporter of your caliber on this beat. You missed a good fundraiser last night. I was there until well after midnight. Perhaps next time."

With that, he signaled to his political ally and strode toward him.

Eww.

She stepped into a deserted part of the hallway and dialed Detective Chaney, knowing he wouldn't take her call. She left a message saying she was hoping for an update on the dead body in the trunk and that she'd call back.

Next, she phoned her editor to say there was nothing new to report from the budget meeting, agreed to tweet a council-continues-to-meet post to the station's website and happily drove back to the crime scene. She'd researched the property records and planned to interview the homeowners and neighbors. People were usually more willing to talk to the news media and own their fifteen minutes of fame than they were to cooperate with the police. Maybe by now the young man she'd seen escorted away by the police was back home. The address came back to a Mr. and Mrs. Sharpei but she couldn't assume he was the owner or even lived there. The police hadn't handcuffed him and they hadn't treated him like a suspect. No charges had been filed yet. She'd checked.

To her dismay, the crime scene remained cordoned off behind yellow police tape and a patrolman sat in his car on the street blocking the driveway. She'd circle back later. She headed for the nearest fast-food restaurant, starving for lunch, and dialed Detective Bentley. No answer. Same message as she left for Chaney.

She called Tessa, bracing herself for the anticipated tirade.

"I get that she's angry, but she doesn't have to take it out on me," Tessa said immediately after answering. "I can't believe she did this to me. I was late for work today. She borrowed my goddamn car and never came home."

"Hello to you too."

"She's not answering my texts. Or my calls. What kind of mother ignores her own daughter, especially after screwing her over?"

Rylee didn't think her mother would ignore her, particularly since she complained they didn't talk often enough. "Your mom is messed up right now, you know that. We've talked about—"

"She's messed up all right. I hate her. I don't care what my dad did to her, she has no right to treat me like this. She better have a good reason for ghosting me. She better be dead."

A cold chill ran up Rylee's spine. But the car this morning wasn't Tessa's. "When was the last time you heard from her?"

"I texted her around midnight, asking when the fuck she was coming home. She said shortly. One fucking word. That was her response. I went to bed but when I woke up this morning and she wasn't there, I texted her again. She sent some lame-ass apology and said she'd be later than she thought. Probably having one more sexcapade with whoever she picked up last night. She said there was money in her bureau drawer and I should use it to call a ride."

Rylee released the air in her lungs. There was no reason to believe Pearl Owens might be the body in the trunk but, for a minute, she feared the worst. If Tessa received a text this morning, it wasn't her.

"Do you know where she was going last night?"

"Out whoring around is all I know." They'd never shared a

typical mother-daughter relationship. Tessa suspected from an early age that her mother was jealous of her, envious of the attention her father lavished on Tessa while cheating on and ignoring Pearl. Tessa had gotten away from the family homestead, going across the country to college in California, landing a job right away and moving into her own apartment. Rylee had visited for a food-laden, heavy alcohol imbibing holiday weekend. Out from under her father's pampering, Tessa matured and fared well.

The economy threw a wrench into her independence. Tessa lost her job and was forced to move back home. She became a different person. By then, her parents were separated and the relationship with her mother even more strained with only the two of them living in the Owens family homestead. Pete Owens moved into a luxurious condo in Mt. Washington, a neighborhood south of the city that offered a stunning view of the Pittsburgh skyline from its mountaintop.

Tessa described it as a playboy's bungalow. She was as bitter and angry as her mother, for different reasons. Her father no longer spoiled her. She worked part-time at the department store while blanketing public relations firms with her resume. But her shortened job tenure limited her opportunities.

"I hope she had a goddamn good time at my expense. What's your schedule like today? I'll need a ride home if you're available. I'm off at nine."

"Sure, no problem. Even if this story I'm chasing keeps me late, I'll pick you up."

"Ooh, anything juicy?"

"I don't know yet. A female was found dead in the trunk of a car early this morning on some guy's property. So far that's all I know."

"Huh. I bet she didn't treat her daughter like shit. Gotta go. See you later."

4

Bentley's heart skittered in a tiny triumphant dance of victory. Her exclamation prompted Chaney to look up from his computer screen.

"Ha! It's a damn rental." She approached his desk with a printout in her hand. "No wonder it was so clean. I told you so. Stolen from the airport holding lot about a month ago."

Chaney groaned. "No tracking data?"

"Disabled. The car is a dead end."

"Same here," he said, indicating the missing person reports he reviewed. "Since at least midnight, no one has missed Jane Doe."

Bentley felt a tug in her chest. "That's rather sad. I'm going to check in on Dickey. Maybe he'll feel sorry for Jane Doe and tell me what he knows."

"Is his lawyer here?"

"No, but he's been sitting in that holding room for most of the morning, waiting on a lawyer who doesn't seem in a hurry to rush to his client's aid. He might be getting a little antsy by now. Maybe I can persuade him to shorten his stay." After all, the room was an interior space with no windows and only a gunmetal table and two chairs. He had to be going stir crazy.

Chaney nodded. "You can try but if he wants to wait for this phantom lawyer, we have no choice." Neither she nor Chaney were familiar with the name Sharpei said would counsel him, which was odd since she knew most of the defense attorneys in the city, even the public defenders.

Chaney winked at her. "Try using your feminine wiles."

She shot him a look that could strip the kernels off an ear of corn, hearing his deep belly laugh as she walked away.

This was a long shot but, until the coroner completed the autopsy, they had no leads. There was no guarantee Dickey would offer any, however, she preferred to be proactive rather than wait for something to break. She hit up the vending machine for a Coke and a bag of chips, knocked on the door just to appear polite, and entered.

"How ya holding up, Dickey?" His eyes were blackened by dark smudges, his hair looked like he'd run his dirty hands through it more than once and his knee bounced non-stop under the table. He grabbed for the pop can.

"D'you hear from my lawyer yet?"

"Not yet. Are you sure your call went through?"

He didn't answer, too busy gulping the soft drink. She tossed the chips toward him and watched him rip open the bag. Eight of his knuckles were tattooed, one hand spelling L-O-V-E and the other, H-A-T-E. The tattoo sleeve crawling up his left arm to his elbow was a hodgepodge of criminal implements—guns, knives, nunchucks, brass knuckles and a few she couldn't identify. The colors were faded, the lines blurred.

"While we're waiting for your attorney, can we go over what you already told us? That can't hurt, right? It's what we already know."

The chips crunched in his mouth.

"You said you were out partying until early this morning. Just one bar or a couple?"

He lifted the can to his mouth.

"I know when I'm out with my friends, we tend to bar hop. See who's out and about and where the best band is playing. Were you doing that last night or did you stay in one place?"

"You party?" His eyes reduced to slits.

She laid her hands on her waist, fingers toward her spine, and arched her back as if to crack it, extending her breasts forward. It was about as sexy as she could get with a bulletproof vest underneath her Pittsburgh Police pullover. "Not around here, I don't. But yeah, I like a good time. I get that you do too. Were you partying with that woman last night?"

"I told you, I never seen her before."

"And you never saw that car before?"

"Never."

She took a deep breath. "Where'd you go last night, Dickey? Who were you with? Anyone who can verify your story? Give you an alibi? You understand it will be to your benefit to give me the names of your buddies and your drinking spots because you're on probation for drug possession and right now, you're our only suspect. This won't go your way unless you help yourself."

"That's bullshit."

"No, that's a fact. You're the only connection to the dead woman."

"I ain't got no connection to her. It was a joke."

"What was?"

He may have been a thug, but he wasn't stupid. She saw it in his stare. But he was nervous. That leg never quieted down.

"What kind of joke? On who?"

"I want my lawyer."

∽

CHANEY THOUGHT she was wasting her time, but the investigation was at a standstill and Bentley needed to move. She drove back to the Sharpei house for another look at the property. The patrolman stationed at the end of the driveway acknowledged her and stayed in his air-conditioned cruiser when she motioned for him to do so. This year seemed like an endless summer. It was going to be another hazy, hot, and humid day, unusual for late August.

The rental car was gone. She stood in the spot it had occupied, her eyes closed. Like the ADA, she believed a crime scene possessed an energy. But the air didn't crackle, didn't crawl up her arms or shiver her spine as other death sites had. Jane Doe wasn't killed here.

The beep of a horn transported her back to the concrete she stood on. Rylee Lapiz waved to her from a fifteen-year-old, dinged Toyota. At least she worked a story, unlike some of her colleagues who rarely left their desks. Rylee claimed that reporters were like police, always searching for the facts. And she maintained there was no news in the newsroom.

Instead of trying to cross the fluttering police tape, Rylee exited her vehicle and leaned against the front fender, waiting for her. Bentley appreciated her respect for the neon yellow barrier.

"There's nothing here for you to see. What are you doing here?"

Lapiz shrugged. "I left messages for you and Detective Chaney. I didn't expect a call back so I thought I might find the homeowners here. Or talk to their neighbors. Any name on the dead woman yet?"

"Not yet.

"Anything at all you can tell me? You know how my editors are."

Yeah, blood thirsty. But Rylee wasn't like them. She'd heard

Rylee say more than once, facts matter. "How about I'm as frustrated as you at the moment."

They both turned when a car drove into the driveway directly across from the Sharpei home. The woman who stepped out of the driver's side wore lilac scrubs and tennis shoes. Her mouth formed a perfect oval, and she shaded her eyes against the afternoon sun as she walked down her drive toward them, cell phone in her hand, her car door hanging open.

"My god, what happened? Are the Sharpeis all right?"

Bentley strode to the middle of the road, retrieved her badge from her back pocket and waited for the woman to reach her and Rylee, who moved up to stand beside her.

"Ma'am, I'm Detective Parker Bentley. There's been an incident here this morning. Can you—"

"What happened? Is everyone all right?" she repeated, her face a shade paler.

"Yes ma'am, the Sharpeis are fine. Were you home last night? Did you see or hear anything suspicious?"

The woman glanced at her badge and refocused on Rylee. Her cheeks wrinkled as her face scrunched. "I know you. You're that reporter from the TV, aren't you?"

Rylee grinned and extended her hand. "Hi, Rylee Lapiz. Always nice to meet a viewer."

The woman shook her hand vigorously. "I watch you every chance I get. Love your reporting. If you say it, I believe it. Tell me, do the anchors have a wardrobe budget? They're always impeccably dressed. I wish I had half their fashion sense."

Rylee nodded. "I know, right? I'm so jealous of them." As she spoke, she motioned to her blue jeans, pocketed T-shirt, and tennis shoes. Bentley had seen Rylee in action before. Lapiz was good at establishing a rapport with the people she interviewed.

She stood barely over five feet and likely weighed one-hundred pounds soaking wet. Her eyes were bright, her smile genuine and her handshake firm. Dressed the way she was, with her dark hair tied into a ponytail, she looked more like a high school senior than a professional newswoman. But Bentley knew she'd graduated with honors and earned a master's degree in journalism. She was no dummy.

The woman was infatuated with Rylee. "It's so nice to see you in our neighborhood. What happened here? Will it be on the six o'clock news?"

Bentley cleared her throat. "Would you mind telling me if you were home last night? Are you just coming home from work now?"

The woman ran her eyes from Bentley's face to her feet, then addressed Rylee again. "Is this breaking news? I love when you reporters say that." Her head dropped back, and she emitted a gleeful laugh toward the sky. "It makes everything so exciting."

Bentley sighed with exasperation, appreciating that Rylee repressed a smile. "It is breaking news and you can be part of the story if you let me and Detective Bentley ask you a few questions."

The woman's shoulders straightened. She released the elastic band holding her hair at her neck. It fell to her shoulders and she fluffed it. "Are there cameras here?"

Rylee smiled. "No, for now I'll use my phone to record your comments. Those will be posted to our website online. A camera crew can come back if you're available later." She punched the red record button on her phone and held it toward the woman. "Were you here last night? Did you see anything unusual?"

Bentley didn't like watching Rylee conduct the interview of a potential witness but Suzy Scrubs was having nothing to do with her.

"No, I worked a twelve-hour shift last night at the hospital. I had an appointment that took all morning so I'm just now getting home." She waved her hand through the air to indicate her ranch home with its manicured lawn and blooming shrubs. Crap. Another dead end.

When the woman asked again what happened Rylee said a body had been found in an abandoned car in the Sharpei driveway.

"No kidding." The woman looked appropriately anxious. "Did you talk to their son, Dickey? He runs with a nasty crowd."

Time for the detective to take over the interview. "How so, ma'am?" Rylee didn't object.

"They're loud, whooping and hollering whenever a car full of them arrives to pick him up. They all look like they need scrubbed down. I smell the stench from whatever wreck they drive up in clear over here. Marijuana for sure." She blushed and clasped her hands against her generous chest. "I know what that smells like. Had a brief wild phase of my own when I was younger. They hurl beer cans out the windows too. They have no respect for people's property."

"Would you be able to recognize any of his friends?"

"Nah, I just see them from my front window. They never get out of the car. Dickey always slinks out the front door, his pants halfway down his ass, his clothes rumpled. His mother can't be very proud."

"Do you know his parents?" She flipped open her iPad. "They didn't seem to be home this morning. Do you know how I can reach them?"

"No idea. Mark and Janet, I think. I rarely see them, but I work odd hours. I hear a lot of yelling when the windows are open and I'm home. The mother's a blonde with big sunglasses. She teeters out the garage door on high heels, waves and drives away. I always wonder if there are black eyes behind those glasses."

"Did you ever witness violence?" She hadn't considered either of them as a possible suspect.

"No, just heard the screaming. I try to mind my own business."

"How about Mr. Sharpei? Ever have contact with him?"

"The few times I've seen him, he's worn a suit and tie. Same as her, nods and drives off. The only reason I'm certain of Dickey's name is because his friends yell for him and lay on the horn. The whole neighborhood knows that kid's name."

"Ma'am, do you have a doorbell camera?"

She looked incredulous. "Of course, I do."

"Would it be possible to review the video from last night?"

Suzy Scrubs looked dubious. "Isn't that an invasion of my privacy?"

Rylee interjected. "Not at all. It's footage we might be able to broadcast. You might be helping solve a murder."

Bentley bristled. "You can't use it if it's evidence, Rylee."

Rylee's smile disappeared. "The hell I can't. This woman, miss...?"

"Ward. Sophie Ward."

"Miss Ward is agreeing to be interviewed by me. You can't forbid her from showing me her camera footage."

"I can ask her not to."

A bark of a laugh turned both their attentions back to Sophie Ward. She pointed her index finger at Bentley.

"Sorry, honey, but no po-leece is telling me what I can and can't do with my own stuff. If it wasn't for her," she aimed her finger at Rylee, "I wouldn't be standing here giving you the time of day. I don't trust cops." Now her hands sat akimbo on her waist. "If Rylee Lapiz wants to look at my doorbell camera, I'm damn well going to show it to her and there isn't anything you can do to stop me. Am I correct?" Her right eyebrow formed a perfect arch.

"Unless, of course, Detective, you want to arrest me for

being uncooperative and then I'll have a hell of a lawsuit against this city and maybe I won't have to work twelve-hour shifts anymore."

"I won't arrest you. I'll just subpoena your camera and you can miss a day of work to testify in court. Now—"

Sophie Ward huffed and Rylee spoke over both of them, raising her hands like an orchestra leader. "Let's take a minute here. Detective Bentley is not the enemy, nor am I. Sophie, it's wonderful to meet someone so community minded. Usually, people are hesitant to be interviewed by a reporter."

That's not what Rylee giggled about the night she was drunk. She told Bentley people would run to line up in front of a camera and practically grab a microphone from her hand to comment on a story, even when they had nothing to say. Rylee knew how to work an interview.

"You can call up the footage right from your phone." Rylee moved beside the woman and walked her through the steps. Bentley moved to her other side, deciding to acquiesce for the moment if it allowed her a look at the street view.

The sun shining over them was a problem.

"Come up on the porch, it will be easier to see." Sophie Ward invited Rylee, but she followed and moved in when Rylee grabbed her forearm to draw her closer.

The time stamp displayed thirty-seven minutes after three in the morning. A shadow of a car moving at a snail's pace, headlights off, slowing down, activated the motion detector light mounted above the Sharpei's garage door. In the darkness, the white Chevy they'd discovered this morning backed into the driveway. An obscure figure emerged from the driver's seat wearing a dark hoodie. It stopped, leaned over near the front right tire, then hustled down the driveway and out of the picture. The person remained hunched over, hood pulled over his head, hands in his pants pockets. Even in broad daylight, an identification was likely impossible.

"Well, whaddaya know," Sophie Ward said.

"May we watch it again?" Rylee sounded like a child asking for a piece of candy. Without waiting for Sophie Ward's approval, her finger touched the replay arrow.

Parker studied the video as it replayed. They rewatched the mysterious driver deposit the car and hurry away. Where was he walking to in the middle of the night? Was there a car waiting for him farther up the street? Perhaps they needed to extend their canvas to view doorbell camera video.

For Bentley, it was a possible lead. For Rylee, it was an exclusive. "Would you be willing to share this with me, Sophie. I can show you how to send it to my phone. Is it the common spelling of your name? S-O-P—"

"Wait a minute, Rylee." Bentley wasn't going to be outmaneuvered by a news reporter.

Rylee's hand flew up. "And also share it with Detective Bentley? She—"

"Ma'am, I—"

Sophie Ward interrupted them. The phone shook in her trembling hand. "I don't know what I just watched but I don't trust the police. I have friends and nephews arrested for no good reasons." She focused on Rylee. "I'll send it to you. What you do with it and who you share it with is your business."

Rylee leveled her gaze on Bentley. "I'll share it with you, Detective, but I'm not suppressing it. If you'd like to comment on the footage, I'll be happy to include that with the broadcast. You can even discredit its validity if you like. Say whatever you want. But we're running with this on the next newscast."

5

Hours later, Rylee waited for Tessa in her car outside the department store. It had been a good day. Thanks to Sophie Ward, her TV station was ahead of all the other media outlets reporting on the Jane Doe murder. Detective Bentley was pissed with Rylee for broadcasting the doorbell footage, but without Rylee, Bentley wouldn't have that small lead. Police officers were now canvasing the adjacent streets searching for any video that showed where the shadowy form disappeared to. There might have been a car waiting for him or her, or they could at least determine the direction the person walked. Without Sophie Ward's delight at meeting Rylee, and her excitement about being on the news, Bentley wouldn't know any of that.

Rylee was friendly with the cops, but they weren't friends. Tomorrow she'd return to the neighborhood and interview Richard "Dickey" Sharpei.

Tessa dropped into the car ass first, tossed a bag at Rylee, then dumped a second one and her purse at her feet. "These were on sale. With my discount, yours was virtually free. That's the only thing I like about this job. That and I don't have to think too hard. Thanks for picking me up."

Rylee eased a multi-colored green shirt from the bag. "Wow, thank you. You didn't have to."

Tessa fanned the air. "I bought one too, in pale blue. I'm starved. Have you eaten yet?"

"Nope. Want to swing through *Smitty's*?" It was Rylee's favorite dive bar on the far side of town that served outstanding food. Plus, Elliott the bartender poured generously. She ate and drank there often enough to know most of the staff by name. It was a comfortable place for a single woman to unwind after a difficult day and it was blocks from her apartment.

"Sounds perfect."

The place was hopping but they squeezed into a table in the corner and ordered steak salads. It sounded healthy, and most times Rylee tried to maintain a sensible diet, but the Pittsburgh tradition of topping the fresh green lettuce, tomato, cooked egg and shredded cheese with crisp French fries and extra ranch dressing was an indulgence she could never resist.

Tessa downed her first mug of beer and ordered a second before their food arrived.

"What's the status with your mom?"

"Don't call her that. If you want to use an M-word, how about monster. Or merciless bitch. Or miserable being. I wouldn't even place human in front of it."

Rylee felt her eyebrows rise. "Jesus, Tessa, I've never seen you so angry."

"I hate her. To ignore me for this long is unacceptable."

"So, you haven't heard from her yet? I'm guessing you tried calling as well as texts?"

"Several times. I'll bet she turned off her phone just to avoid me."

"Did you ask your dad if he's heard from her?"

"No, why would he? Those two barely communicate

anymore. I don't know why my father refuses to sign divorce papers. He could be rid of her. And then I'd be done with her, too."

A divorce wouldn't look good on Peter Owens' resume. Rylee dove into her salad, her taste buds salivating the second the waitress laid the bowl in front of her. Tessa ordered a third beer and a second for her.

"Didn't you buy one of those tags that allows you to locate your car? You used it last Saturday after that concert in the park. You told me it was worth every penny you spent because you were tipsy and it led you right to your parking spot. Did you try that?"

Tessa's fork stopped in mid-air. "I'm not stupid, you know. I did but it's not working."

"How can it not be working? You just bought it."

She shrugged. "I don't know. You know I'm not good with technology gizmos. I tried it this morning and nothing. Maybe the battery died. Whatever. I can't locate the car."

Rylee held out her hand. "Give me your phone. The thing is brand new. It worked on Saturday. This is Wednesday. The battery can't be dead."

She punched in Tessa's birthday to unlock Tessa's phone and tapped the appropriate button. Nothing. She tried a second time. "This is really odd. It should work."

"I don't know. Maybe the bitch knows how to disable it so I can't find her."

Tessa might not be worried but Rylee sure was.

A string of curse words that rose above the normal din of the bar caught Rylee's attention. It was Richard Sharpei from this morning, surrounded by several men who were apparently disputing something he said.

"Holy shit, that's the guy who was at the crime scene this morning."

Tessa turned in the direction she looked.

"His name is the same as the listed homeowner. Could be a son or a brother. He was at the house and made the discovery. I watched the police take him away. He must not be a suspect or he wouldn't be out partying with his buds. I was planning to find him tomorrow but maybe he'll talk to me now."

"Now? While you're here having dinner with me?"

Tessa's comment surprised her. She choked up a laugh, trying to brush off Tessa's attitude. "It's not like we're on a date. It will only take a few minutes."

"I'm in the middle of a crisis and all you can think about is your nose for news. I really hate you sometimes." She yanked her phone from her purse and began tapping the screen.

"What the hell? What's the matter with you?" Dumbfounded, Rylee watched her friend crush her napkin into a wad and drop it on her unfinished sandwich, gulp the rest of her beer and stand.

"I've called a ride. Thanks for nothing."

Rylee closed her open mouth. That was out of the blue. She'd seen Tessa pitch temper tantrums before but she'd never said I hate you. It stung a little. Tomorrow, Tessa would call and apologize like always. In one way, Pearl Owens was right. Tessa was spoiled and entitled, thanks to her father's copious attentions. If her mom didn't return her car soon, it wouldn't surprise Rylee if her dad gifted her with a new one.

Maybe Rylee would call her police contacts and ask if there were any abandoned vehicles discovered. She didn't know Tessa's license number but she knew the model and color. Meanwhile, she'd finish her salad, allow Mr. Sharpei to have another round, then see if he'd talk to her.

Sharpei and his buddies were a raucous bunch, lobbing fries at each other and sticking them up their nose, talking over one another, and dropping F-bombs like crazy. Rylee used the ladies' room and zipped her tote. The designer tote had been a gift from Tessa. Rylee was certain TSA agents would classify it as luggage. It regularly held her notebooks, extra pens, her laptop, various personal items like a toothbrush and toothpaste, deodorant and cologne for days when she didn't feel fresh and sometimes, a clean shirt if she knew she was going out for happy hour right after work. It was heavy enough to use as a battering ram. She hefted it onto her shoulder and walked up to the group of five. Her arrival silenced them momentarily.

"Richard Sharpei? Hi, I'm Rylee Lapiz from Channel 5 news." She extended her hand, ignoring the whistles and catcalls from his friends. "I was at your house this morning when the police were there. Would you mind if I asked you a few questions?"

Up close and personal, the kid wasn't a pleasant sight. Bloodshot eyes, stringy hair, fingernails caked with dirt and a faint body odor. His palm was sweaty and his handshake weak.

"I seen you on TV, ain't I?"

She forced a smile and uttered her standard line when meeting prospective interviewees or wannabes. "Always nice to meet a viewer."

"You gonna put me on TV?" His buddies clapped him on the back, whooped and hollered.

"Dickey's gonna be a star."

"Way to go, Dickey."

"Smile for the camera, Dickey."

Elliott appeared at the bar. "Everything okay here, hun?"

She nodded. "So far. But don't go on break." He flashed a quick smile, gathered their empty whiskey glasses, and walked away.

"Mr. Sharpei, could I ask you about—"

"*Mister* Sharpei," his friend shrieked. "Who the fuck does she think you are?" Another friend tapped his forehead, his lips, his chest and bowed, reciting "All hail Mister Sharpei."

Dickey simply stared at her.

She'd learned early in her career to ignore the ass hats. She was young, petite, and fairly attractive, although her lips were too small and her nose crooked. But being not bad looking often was a disadvantage. To a woman like Sophie Ward, she was a girl struggling to make a career. To degenerates like Dickey's friends, she was a conquest to be made.

She leveled her shoulders and looked him dead in the eye. "I saw you leave with the police this morning, Mr. Sharpei. You weren't handcuffed so I assume they didn't arrest you. You wouldn't be here tonight if they had."

He sneered. "How do you know? Maybe I got a good lawyer."

"Can you tell me who that is?"

His head jerked. "What do you want with him? I thought you wanted to talk to me?"

"Yes sir, I—" More whoops and whistles from his entourage, still amused by the title. "I very much would like to talk to you. Did you have information you shared with the police? Are you their key witness to cracking this case?" Might as well blow a little sunshine up his ass.

"I ain't a witness to anything."

"Well, then, what did the police want to talk to you about? What did you tell them?"

"Lady, if a dead woman was found in your driveway, don't you think the po-po would want to talk to you too? I thought you were smart. You seem smart on TV."

"You're right, that was a dumb question. What can you tell me about the dead woman in the car? Did you know her? Do you know how she died?"

His friends held make believe microphones in his face, one using a pretzel rod, one a French fry, and one a fork. She ignored them.

"The police report is public record. I already read it." It was a barebones report, listing only his name, address, and age but he didn't know that. "May I call you Dickey? The report only gives me half the story, Dickey. The cops' half. I'd rather hear what you have to say."

"I ain't talkin' on TV."

"You don't have to, sir." More noise that she ignored. She located her phone in her purse, pressed voice memos and the red record button and held it in her hand. In Pennsylvania, it is illegal to record a conversation unless all parties are informed they are being taped. She wasn't going to spell it out for Dickey, but the phone was in plain sight, the counter running. With all the noise in the bar, it might not pick up the conversation but jotting notes in her notebook didn't seem like a good idea right now. It might spook him.

"Just tell me what you know. It can be on background, if you like. I—"

"What's that mean?"

"You would just be filling me in on the details that you know. Whatever you can tell me. Did you know the woman?"

"If I did, I would'na been able to recognize her. She had no face left." She nodded as if she'd seen it too. From the look on his face, she was grateful she hadn't. He lifted his beer with a trembling hand and slurped. His eyes widened and his friends grew quieter. "I never seen nothin' like that. Man, somebody did a number on her."

"Were you the one who found her?"

"Yeah. Scared me shitless. The minute I saw that car in the driveway, I knew it was bad news."

"Why? What made you so suspicious? Did you recognize the car?"

"No, I never seen it. That's what I told the police, too. But there was talk, you know, about what to do if I ever found a car in my driveway like that."

"Talk? What kind of talk? Who talked about it?"

One of Dickey's friends held up his hand. "I ain't part of this. I'm outta here." Dickey stared after him as he walked away. She couldn't let that break his momentum.

"Who talked about something like that, Dickey? What were you supposed to do when you found the car?"

Dickey glared at her. "I can't talk to you. This is big shit, bigger than you and your TV show."

"You can talk to me off the record. I don't need to use your name or identify you in any way. Tell me what you know about finding that car. No one will know we spoke."

He shifted from foot to foot. "I don't know nothin', I told you."

One of his friends tugged on his arm. "Let's go."

She signaled for Elliott. "Let me buy you and your friends another round. Just chat with me a bit. Let's talk about a hypothetical situation where a man discovers a strange car in his driveway and no one else is around. What's he supposed to do about it?

"Elliott, another round for these gentlemen, on my tab, please." Free drinks for Dickey and his friends bought her a little time. "It's an imaginary scenario, an upstanding member of the community finds an unknown vehicle in his driveway one morning. What does he do?"

Dickey shot the whiskey and gulped half of his fresh brew. "He doesn't do what they expect him to, I'll tell you that."

She gasped. "What's he supposed to do?"

He glared at her so long, she was certain he wouldn't answer. He drained the mug. "Get rid of it. Not call the fuckin' police. I fucked up big time but I ain't takin' the rap for him. I wrote shit down, you know? Just in case. He comes after me, I got a, whaddaya call it, a record. I ain't as dumb as he thinks." He slammed the empty glass on the bar and pointed a grimy finger at her face. "Put that on your TV station. Dickey ain't goin' down for this."

Before she could ask another question, he shoved past her and strode out the door, his gait a little unsteady. He was drunk and possibly a little high. Was he going to drive? She wanted to run after him, but his escorts stared her down, one of his friends holding up his index finger and swishing it back and forth like a windshield wiper. They waited until Dickey was out the door, then filed out behind him. No big deal. Tomorrow morning she'd knock on his front door. Without his gang to embolden him, Dickey might be a little more forthcoming.

Elliott gathered the empty liquor glasses. "He's not exactly your type, hun. What was all that about?"

She switched off her phone, frowning. "He has something to do with a dead woman. I was trying to get an interview. Is he a regular here? I haven't seen him here before."

"Tonight's the first time for that crew to show up here. Usually they drink at *The Last Sip Saloon*. That's not a place you want to go, especially not alone."

She wrinkled her nose. *The Last Sip Saloon* was in a seedier section of the city, known for drug deals and drive-by shootings. "That's not your kind of hangout either. What were you doing there?"

Elliott's impish grin lit up his eyes. "My cousin bar tends there. He's the black sheep of the family, involved in unsavory activities." He arched his right eyebrow. "But I like him and some nights I sub for him to give him time off." Both his hands went up. "I don't ask what he does with that time. Even he says it's better that I don't know."

"Huh. Well, if I can't find Dickey tomorrow, maybe you can put me in touch with your cousin and he can help. Thanks for looking out for me tonight." She blew him a kiss. They shared a mutual attraction that they'd tried to capitalize on, but Elliott worked nights and Rylee worked days and nights. He was philosophical about their schedules, believing that their stars would align someday. She figured it would happen when the TV station went out of business or hell froze over.

She couldn't afford time for a relationship anyway. Competition at work was cutthroat, everybody aiming for the next big headline and subsequent promotion to anchor broadcasting. The station was fourth in the market but its ratings were climbing. In part, her bosses said, because of their response to breaking news. Most of the time, it involved police activity and her presence. Her job left her no life but she thrived on it. She had no desire to sit behind the news desk at noon or dinnertime and smile while someone else reported from the scene of a big story. She'd wither there. She belonged in the trenches. Her heart was in the hunt for the facts. That ambition wasn't healthy for a relationship. Look how Tessa reacted tonight.

She turned the ignition in her car and rehashed Tessa's outburst. It had come from left field and, admittedly, hurt Rylee's feelings. She had two people to follow up with tomorrow, her best friend and Dickey Sharpei.

6

Bentley cursed under her breath and flipped Chaney the bird when he snorted a laugh.

Seven in the morning on a Saturday and the phone message light was already blinking. They weren't on the Saturday rotation today but this case took priority over a weekend off. And who knows how many calls would be waiting if she didn't check until Monday.

The Tip Line had been her idea. They were at a loss as to Jane Doe's identity. No one had reported a missing woman between the ages of fifty to sixty. That was the coroner's estimated age for Jane Doe.

About five-feet-four-inches and, as Parker suspected, a brunette. She'd given birth at least once and was in reasonably good health. The only identifiable stomach content was red wine. Lots of it, according to the autopsy report. Enough to be way over the legal limit. Flat out drunk. Unable to adequately defend herself from her attacker.

She'd endured a heck of a beating, suffering broken ribs, a punctured lung, kidney damage—the coroner suspected she'd been kicked multiple times—a broken jaw and fractured eye socket. No sign of sexual assault. Her red lace panties matched her bra. Bentley only coordinated her underwear when she had a date, a statement she absently made to Chaney's delight.

She'd spent two days fielding tip line calls, more like falling down rabbit holes, and so far nothing had been useful.

"No, ma'am, this isn't a number to refer you to the best bakery in town. I don't eat donuts."

"Yes sir, a barking dog is an annoyance, but this isn't where you report the nuisance. I'll refer this to an officer from your zone and someone will be in touch."

"No sir, no aliens were reported in the area, but we'll keep a look out."

Chaney advised her to let all the calls go to the voice mailbox so she could weed out the whackos, but she was a hands-on investigator. Except when the phone rang again, she kept her hands off.

"Was I naïve to think someone would actually call with credible information?"

Chaney shook his head. "Let's call it optimistic. C'mon. You need a break and we were just summoned to a shoot fest on the east side. Happened early this morning but the uniforms on scene specifically invited us to the party."

"To a drive-by? How come? We're not on the rotation."

Chaney shrugged his answer.

Bentley wasn't as compliant. "I don't understand how the hell we are supposed to work a case that ADA Moore deems a priority if we keep getting assigned other cases to work at the same time?"

Chaney grinned. "Ah, did the dragon lady call you again asking for a progress report?"

"Yes, and I wanted to tell her we're not fucking miracle workers. It takes time."

Chaney tossed her the keys. "Welcome to the real world, Detective. Crime doesn't wait for your schedule to accommodate it. Part of being a detective is juggling cases, switching between wildly different gears. You'll learn."

"But there's so much to do on the Jane Doe case. The new doorbell camera footage has to be reviewed. I submitted a request to the traffic division to check their street cameras. That Chevy didn't drop from the sky into Dickey Sharpei's driveway. If I can backtrack its entry, maybe I can find where it started. I can't do any of that if I have to chase a drive-by shooting. It's probably a drug deal gone bad, a case for narcotics to pursue. Why call us? Are there fatalities?"

"I don't know details, only that we were requested at the scene." Chaney patted her shoulder. "That's a good idea about the traffic cams. You should ask someone from IT to help otherwise you'll spend hours in front of that computer screen. Let's see what this call involves and maybe I can free you up to work Jane Doe and I'll chase this one."

The compromise appeased her temporarily. When she wore a uniform, cases belonged to the officer responding to the call. Rarely did she have multiple open investigations. With only sixteen city detectives in the bureau working any given shift, the criminals outnumbered the crime solvers.

It had been an unusually hot summer and isolated homicides led to a death toll on pace to be the highest in the city in decades. Domestic violence was a primary cause, followed closely by shootings driven by arguments that escalated from social media posts. The east side of town had a disproportionate share of fatalities.

Sergeant Cubb greeted them outside *The Last Sip Saloon*, shaking their hands. "Sorry to bother you. This appeared to be nothing more than a rowdy, end-of-summer drive-by. No one injured, nothing damaged. Most of our intel is that this area is neutral territory. No gang activity so we ruled that out immediately. Our sources confirm all sides seem to be taking the summer off." He pointed them toward the side of the building and talked as they walked.

"The call came in at three-seventeen this morning. The bar was closed, according to the owner, but folks were still milling around outside. Can't blame them. The temperature was pleasant last night, and the sky was clear. A perfect night to party. There won't be many more of those. The first unit on scene secured the premises and began interviews. Most everyone came out of their home once the lights and sirens arrived so they called for additional manpower. I got here about an hour ago."

Bentley looked around at the gawkers. Didn't people in this neighborhood sleep in on the weekend? She refocused on Cubb. "If no one was injured, why call us?"

Cubb held up his index finger. "Everyone says they were here but no one saw anything. What a surprise, huh?" He pointed west. "A car drove by from that direction, unloading a clip in the air. Nothing and no one hit out front. Not even a window broken, which I find odd. On the surface, it seemed like a noisy joy ride.

"I walked this perimeter looking for spent shells or anything I could find that might be helpful." He motioned for them to follow. "I don't know what drew me here to the back but I followed the fence around the rear of the building. It's a small piece of property, barely large enough to hold those two dumpsters. That's when I spotted the tennis shoes, behind the smaller bin, not flat like they'd been discarded but on the heels at an awkward angle. It's your boy from the other day, Sharpei."

Bentley blustered. "What? Are you sure? Is he dead?"

Cubb lifted the latch on the chain link gate and the trio moved toward the overflowing metal dumpsters. Garbage was strewn all around the bins, so full the lids couldn't close. Chaney coughed and Bentley gagged from the odor. As soon as the sun came up, flies would swarm the contents. Wedged behind a ten-yard bin lay Dickey Sharpei, his eyes blackened, his shirt bloodied from a broken nose and the hole in the middle of his forehead.

Bentley's heart sank. "Fuck."

Chaney knelt in the beams of their flashlights. "You got any gloves?"

Cubb handed him and Bentley a pair of black nitrile gloves.

Chaney checked for a pulse, even though it was apparent Sharpei was dead. "Rigor mortis has already set in. He's been dead at least four hours. He wasn't caught in the drive-by?"

"How could he have been?" Bentley asked, leaning over his shoulder while holding the back of her hand against her nose. "All the gunfire was out front. No one has invented a bullet yet that can navigate its way around a building."

Chaney looked at Cubb. "Shot out front and dragged around here?"

"Doubtful. The group would have scattered if anyone had gone down. The drive-by was the highlight of their night."

Chaney searched Dickey's pockets while he asked, "Why didn't the bar crew see him when they took the trash out after closing?"

Cubb shrugged. "A few of the staff were still here when our units arrived. Some of their friends were among the crowd hanging outside. I—"

"Was the owner still here?" Chaney interrupted.

"No, but after I found your boy," Cubb nodded toward Sharpei, "I called him and asked him to come back. He doesn't live too far from here. He's in the office inside along with the rest of the staff who worked last night. He called them all back in. They've all been cooperative and a little upset. Sharpei was a regular here.

"No one saw anything suspicious," Cubb continued. "Two men hauled the garbage bags out here around two-thirty. They swear the body wasn't here. In fact, one of the men knocked that cardboard box out of the bin and picked it up from the ground. Judging from its position on top of the heap, it would have fallen right at Sharpei's feet."

Bentley touched Cubb's arm. "So, either he's lying or Dickey was dumped here after closing. What was your gut instinct about him?"

"Truthful."

She typed on her iPad. "That means Dickey was killed somewhere else. Super. Another goddamn body and no crime scene. The drive-by could have been a diversion. Grab everyone's attention out front while you dump Dickey in back."

Cubb agreed. "It's possible."

Chaney rose, folding the gloves into themselves as he removed them. "Pockets are empty. No ID. No cell phone. There isn't a twenty-five-year-old on this planet who doesn't have a cell phone with him at all times. Maybe we can ping its location. Anybody else been back here?"

Cubb shook his head. "No sir. I kept everyone out front. Didn't even tell my team. The minute I recognized him, I called you two. I also notified the coroner's office. They're en route. What's protocol? Does the district attorney's office get a call before normal business hours because I sure don't want to be the one to wake up ADA Moore. Especially on a weekend."

"Me neither," Chaney piped up. Both of them leveled their gazes on her.

Bentley aimed her iPad to snap a photo of Dickey. "What's the matter, boys, afraid of the alpha dog?" Their grins were sheepish.

She looked toward Chaney and he held out his hand, palm up as if waiting for a cash tip. "What now, Detective?"

"We interview the employees who were here last night to collect our facts. My theory is that Dickey's death is directly connected to Jane Doe but how do we prove it when he claimed he didn't know her? Maybe the workers inside have some insight. Maybe the two of them drank here together. Let's at least have that much detail in hand before we call Laquisha.

"Wayne, you don't mind, if we re-interview them, do you? I'll review your report when you submit it, but I'd like to talk to them myself, get a feel for how they feel."

Cubb smiled. "Of course, Parker, I'd expect nothing less."

"Will you stay here and keep Dickey company until the coroner arrives? There's a beer in it for you later." His smile grew wider and he agreed.

Chaney eyed her as they walked to the back door of the saloon. "You seem rather chummy with Sergeant Cubb. Anything you care to tell me?"

She couldn't contain her grin. "Not really. We hooked up for a beer the other night to discuss Jane Doe. He's smart and he treats me like you. He respects my opinions."

"Hooked up as in hooked up under the sheets?"

She jabbed his shoulder and grasped the door handle. "A lady doesn't kiss and tell."

Chaney mumbled when Laquisha Moore's car drove through the alley. "Guess it was too much to hope she'd stay in her lane." The string of curse words she spewed would make a truck driver blush. She arrived at the saloon shortly after Bentley called, dressed in blue jeans, a Polo shirt and tennis shoes. The scowl on her face matched Chaney's and backed everyone up except Bentley.

"How in the goddamn hell did this happen?" She could have breathed fire. Chaney and Cubb retreated farther and disappeared through the gate.

"He wasn't a witness, per se, Laquisha. There was no indication he needed protection."

"Who the fuck made that decision?"

Bentley filled her lungs. "He told us he had nothing to do

with Jane Doe. His attorney made the same assurances. He presented as a scared young punk, not someone afraid for his life."

She snorted. "Remind me never to ask you to assess a suspect."

Bentley wanted to remind her that Dickey wasn't a suspect but this was an argument she couldn't win. Sometimes it was better to take the dressing down and move on.

No immediate clues were discovered around his body. Like Jane Doe, he was killed somewhere else and deposited here. Bentley couldn't help but wonder if someone was supposed to dispose of him like Jane Doe and this was their method. If so, it was a poor one.

She and Chaney spent an hour inside the saloon, learning little more than they already knew about Dickey. He ran with a rowdy crowd, used and likely trafficked drugs although no one admitted they knew that as a fact, was a regular at the bar and had to frequently be carried out by his friends and driven home. Not only was he falling down drunk, Dickey didn't drive. The wait staff wasn't particularly fond of him—he didn't tip—but none of them wished him dead.

She found Chaney coming out of the men's room, grimacing. "Don't go in there, it's like a science experiment gone bad." He removed another pair of gloves and tossed them in a can beside the bar.

Bentley sighed. "Miz Moore blames us for not protecting Dickey. She—"

"That's uncalled for." Chaney's face turned red. "If the little shit hadn't lied to us, he might not be dead."

"I hear ya. I'm just giving you the ADA's mood. She's unhappy with our fact-gathering skills. She's requested we take a better look at the area."

"Who the fuck does she think she is?" She could almost see Chaney's blood pressure rise. "She's not our boss. She doesn't tell us what to do. This is the second time she's stepped into our crime scene." He jabbed his thumb into his chest. "Ours, not hers. She doesn't belong here and she sure as hell doesn't tell us how to do our jobs."

Bentley's head bobbed in agreement and she laid her hand on his arm. "I know, I know. But you know she's combatting the odds of being a black woman fighting her way to the top in a man's arena. She's overstepping, yes, but that's her way. It's nothing against us personally."

Chaney snapped. "This isn't about skin color, it's about expertise in the field. My expertise as an investigator. And yours. I don't care what she wants, we're handling this case on our terms."

Daylight had arrived with bright sunshine and the lights set up by the fire department around the perimeter of the crime scene still shined as bright as high noon. They'd already done a thorough search.

Chaney lowered his voice. "It's a waste of our time to search this grid again. Ask Cubb to do it. Did any of the employees here identify Sharpei's friends?"

Bentley exhaled. "If you can call it that. Only first names, and some of those nicknames." She checked her iPad. "There's Tiny, I'm betting he's a larger man. Squirrel. Hector. The bus boy thought his last name might be Santiago. Tommy, also known as Tommy the Thumb, and Angel. I'll search the files for the aliases. Maybe that will give us legal names and known associates. How that will lead us to Dickey's killer or Jane Doe's, I have no idea."

Chaney poked the fingers on his left hand into the palm of his right, forming the letter T. "Time out. Before you do that, we should notify Dickey's parents. Maybe they know who their kid hung out with or what he was into."

"I didn't think of that. I planned to interview them anyway about Jane Doe ending up in their driveway. We automatically assumed Dickey had something to do with her, but who knows, she could have been one of their friends." Seeing the face Chaney made she added, "It's unlikely. But maybe Dickey spilled his guts to them. If they were keeping a secret to protect their kid, for whatever reason, this might break their silence. A closer look at mom and dad won't hurt. Maybe they knew who had it in for Dickey. It's a shitty way to gain information but we don't have much of a choice."

Chaney nodded. "I hate family notifications. It never gets easier. It's still too early. Let's get breakfast first."

7

Rylee stood on the riverbank muttering "Holy shit. Hol-lee shit."

What a way to start her Monday. Her heart raced as fast as her fingers typed on her phone screen, detailing a vehicle extraction.

That's how it had broadcast over the police scanner. A pedestrian walking to work across the Sixth Street Bridge to the North Side saw a car submerged in the water.

She'd arrived just as the tow barge was dragging the red Mustang from the depths of the Allegheny River. Her morning coffee soured in her stomach.

"Hol-lee shit." It was Tessa's car. No license plate, but she recognized the clump of pink, green and blue Mardi Gras beads hanging from the rearview mirror. Tessa proudly told anyone who would listen that she'd earned them legitimately, by displaying her bare breasts to a crowd. Rylee always cringed when she repeated the story.

She hastily texted Tessa. **Where are you? Any word from your mom?**

Dear Lord, was her mother in the driver's seat? Rylee

strained to see and when she couldn't, she walked toward Nick Coooper, a beat cop she was friendly with.

"Hey, Nick."

He greeted her warmly. "Ryyyleee, my favorite reporter. I should've known you'd be here. When are you going to meet me for a drink instead of always at a crime scene?"

He'd asked her out more than once but as long as her assignment was reporting on the cops and the courts, dating him would be unethical. He was one of the kindest men she dealt with, and not bad in the looks department. He filled out a uniform nicely. Neatly trimmed dark hair, gray eyes, and a straight, white smile. It was hard not to smile when he flashed that grin. He was always respectful toward her, not insulting as a few of his coworkers could be. She liked him. But even seeing him secretly wouldn't sit right with her.

She touched his arm. "As soon as one of us gets a different job, I promise. Do you know if there is anyone in the car?" She caught her lip between her teeth, waiting for his response.

"Not to my knowledge. There was no obvious body but you never—what's the matter?"

"That's my friend's car."

He squared his shoulders, the casual air between them morphing into a professional inquiry. "Are you certain? There's no license plate. What's your friend's name?"

"I'm sure. I recognize the beads in the front window and the peace sign stuck to the back bumper. My friend, Tessa Owens, said her mother borrowed her car a couple of days ago and hasn't returned it. She's angry with her mother about it."

Nick's brows furrowed. "Owens, as in Pete Owens, the car dealer and political bigwig?"

"Yep. Tessa is his daughter."

"Crap, that adds a layer of pressure to this shit show." He tapped the microphone attached to the epaulet on his shirt.

"Rescue One, I have a possible identification as to ownership of the vehicle. Any signs of occupancy?"

Rylee held her breath. Tessa hadn't replied to her text.

"Negative so far," came the response.

Her cheeks puffed as she exhaled.

"Give me your friend's name and contact info please. What did her mother tell her about the car?'

"That's just it," Rylee said, scrolling through her contacts. "Her mother has been ghosting her."

"What do you mean?"

"Tessa has texted and tried to call her, but her mom isn't answering. That's why I panicked when I realized it was Tessa's car. Her mom was going out partying—"

"When?'

She handed Nick her phone. "Here, just share the contact to your number. Tessa might be at work today. I don't know her schedule."

Nick tapped her screen as he spoke. "When did she borrow the car?"

Rylee pressed her fingers into her forehead to sidetrack the beginnings of a headache. "Last Tuesday, I think. I'm not sure. Tessa was bitching about it Wednesday night. You'll have to verify it with her."

"What kind of relationship do they have? Would her mother be mean enough to ditch the car in the river? I've met Mr. Owens but never his wife."

Rylee shook her head. "I'm not surprised. They're separated and squaring off for a nasty divorce. Tessa is caught in the middle and resents her mother even more than she already had."

"They don't get along?"

"That's an understatement."

He returned her phone. "I added my personal cell to your contacts. Just in case you decide to take me up on my offer." His smile eased the tension in her shoulders, and she could swear his eyes twinkled.

The car dropped onto the flatbed with a loud bang, water pouring out from its doors and the trunk. They watched a uniformed officer inspect the inside and pop the trunk. Everyone on the channel heard the radio call that the car was unoccupied.

Rylee checked her phone again. Still no return text. "How soon will you contact Tessa?"

"If she's the registered owner, within the hour, why?"

"It might be in her dad's name. I want to post on the station's website about the discovery. I won't identify the owner until the department's information officer confirms it, but if she sees the headline before you guys talk to her or her dad, she'll know I was here and she'll be mad at me."

"For doing your job?"

"Yeah, she doesn't understand me or my commitment to reporting the facts."

His face wrinkled to one side, closing his right eye. "Doesn't sound like much of a friend. You're damn good at what you do."

Few people took the time to tell her that. Her stomach somersaulted. "Thanks, I appreciate that."

He laid his hand lightly between her shoulders. "Before you post anything, let's go chat with the supervisor on scene. That way, it's official."

As they walked, she texted Tessa again. "**Must talk ASAP. Call me.**"

There wasn't much she could tell the supervisor beyond knowing Tessa's contact information, where she worked, and when she believed her mother had borrowed the car.

Rylee didn't have Pearl Owens' new cell number since separating from her husband and being removed from the Owens' account but she provided Peter's. His number was in her political candidates address book. The more she thought about it, the car was probably registered in his name. Tessa couldn't afford to buy a car, and she'd mentioned that her dad had worked a deal. Well hell, the man was a car dealer. It was probably some sort of tax write off, which meant free.

"That's all assumption on my part, remember," she reminded the supervisor.

Nick walked her to her car. "Thanks for your help."

"Will you let me know when ownership has been verified so I can reach out to Mr. Owens for a comment? It won't come from you, I'll verify it with the PIO. But I hate to nag him if the confirmation is slow, especially because I know the information on my own."

"Sure thing. It will give me an excuse to call you."

She unlocked her car and then had a notion. "Would you mind doing me a favor tonight?"

His face brightened.

"I want to track down someone about another story and his hangout isn't in the best neighborhood. I tried to find him earlier today but no one was at his home. I left my card in the door but it's a fat chance he'll call. Is it possible you could meet me there," she held up her hand, "not as a date but more of a backup? Just in case?"

"Where are you going?"

The Last Sip Saloon.

"Jesus, Rylee, that's no place for you to go. I don't care how important the story is. The station is sending you there alone?"

"It's not an assignment. More like research on my own. I've heard the place is a real sewer pit. That's why I'm asking you to be there, not in uniform, in plain clothes, and not really with me but there for me. I'm going to go whether you volunteer or not. It was just a thought I had that maybe going alone isn't smart."

He propped his hands on his hips. "It's not. What's smart is asking for company. What time will you be there and what's in it for me if I do this?"

Her jaw dropped momentarily. "How about a thank you?"

His eyes shone. "How about that drink somewhere nicer when you're finished. One drink, no strings. You can pick up the tab and write it off as a business expense if that makes you more comfortable. It's the only way I'm showing up tonight."

She doubted that but she relented. After all, the idea of spending time with him wasn't repulsive and he *was* doing her a favor. "Okay. One drink. You can buy. Meet me there at ten, please."

He opened her car door. "Am I supposed to know you or ignore you?"

"Ignore me. Just keep an eye on me."

"With pleasure."

She drove away from the scene smiling.

An hour later, she'd reported the identity of the owner of the submerged car but hadn't been able to contact Tessa or Pete Owens for comment. Tessa was acting just like Pearl. She wasn't returning any of Rylee's texts. The day passed without a return call from Peter Owens or a word from Tessa. Nick was right, she thought as she parked in *The Last Sip Saloon's* dirt parking lot. Tessa wasn't a great friend.

She scanned the parking lot for him, hoping as she walked inside that he was there. She didn't spot him but the men who had been with Dickey Sharpei at *Smitty's* were off to one side of the bar, whooping it up as usual. Elliott was not tending bar. Was that his cousin pouring drinks?

They greeted her with whistles and catcalls but quieted when she stopped in front of them.

"Hi, I'm looking for Dickey. Is he here?"

One of them stepped up behind her and placed his hand on the bar, effectively blocking her with his body. He smelled like he needed a shower. "We ain't seen him tonight, sweet thing, but *I* can tell you plenty of stories. What d'you wanna hear?" His breath in her face was sour. His friends found amusement in his bravado.

The bar smelled like sweat and stale beer. The ceiling tiles were black with cigarette smoke. Didn't they ever clean in here?

She breathed through her mouth. "Do you expect him to join you? Or do you know if I can find him somewhere else, maybe another bar?"

A second man, as big as an ape and just as foreboding, stepped into her space. "He might be out back smoking a joint. Want to come out back with us and look for him?" He reached to touch her shoulder and she smacked his hand away. Her heart beat a little faster with the realization that this wasn't a good idea.

"No thanks. If you see him, tell him Rylee Lapiz is looking for him." She laid her business card on the bar. "If he calls me, I'll meet him somewhere." She stepped to her right when the other two apes stood up, grinning as they formed a ring around her. She dropped her left hand into her oversized tote.

"What's your hurry," Sour Breath asked. "Why don't you have a drink with us? Maybe Dickey'll show up." Ape Number One moved closer. Not only was he huge, he had a spider in a web tattooed on a neck so thick it rivaled his biceps.

Where the hell was Nick? She flattened her hand against Ape Number One's chest and shoved. "No, thank you. I have to go."

Caught off guard, he fell backward into a chair, cursing. Ape Number Two stepped toward her and she braced herself. "Listen you baboon, lay one hand on me and I'll cover your face with pepper spray." She eased the bright pink spray cylinder from her bag and positioned her finger on the nozzle.

A deep voice from behind them cut the tension. "You'd best listen to her, boys, she'll do it without thinking twice. She's a man eater."

All eyes turned to Nick standing an arm's length away at the high-top table beside them, tilting back his bottle of beer. He winked at Rylee but it didn't calm her racing heart.

She pushed Ape Number Two backward and moved out of their circle. "Please tell Dickey I'm looking for him," she said over her shoulder as she walked away. She was shaking but she held her head high and her back straight. She didn't look to see if Nick followed her, just plowed her way to the door.

Once outside she stopped, clamped her eyes closed and bent over at the waist. That was stupid.

"Are you going to throw up?" Nick's warm baritone voice spread over her back like butter.

She whirled around. "Some back up you are. I almost got attacked in there. Where were you?" She pointed to the bar as if he didn't know where she'd just been. Her hand shook. The emotion in her voice surprised him, judging by the way his eyebrows shot up.

He reached for her extended arm. "Relax, sweetheart, I was right behind you the whole time. I wasn't going to let anything happen to you." He enfolded her in his arms. "Hey, you're shaking. C'mon, you're tougher than those jerks in there."

She relaxed against him, a bit taken aback by the effect the incident had on her. And the manly way he smelled. His cologne was woodsy. She spoke into his chest with a calmer voice. "I'm sorry, that really scared me." She eased out of his arms and playfully jammed his chest with her forefinger. "Where the hell were you? Some knight in shining armor you turned out to be. I had to save myself."

His laugh was rich and came from deep in his belly as he dropped his arm around her shoulder and they moved toward her car. "Right, so the next time you encounter those assholes, they'll know you're not some weakling who needs rescued. They know you can handle yourself. Nice job with the pepper spray, by the way. Too bad you didn't use it. I would've liked to have seen that big one go down."

She wiped her runny nose with the back of her hand. "We're you there the whole time?"

"From the second you walked in. You said to ignore you so I did but I followed you to them and waited to see what would happen. Any time you need backup, I'm your man. Who's Dickey?"

She exhaled, calmer now. "Dickey Sharpei. He might have information about the dead woman who was found in the trunk of a car the other day. Did you hear about that?"

He had. "Why would he know anything?"

"The car was left in his driveway. I saw the police talking to him and I briefly talked to him the night it happened but he was surrounded by those goons and didn't tell me much. I was hoping to get more information out of him tonight."

"Was that your boss's suggestion, sending you to a place like this at night?"

"No, it was strictly my idea. No one but you knows I'm here."

"You'd make a good cop. Even though that was risky, my respect for you as a reporter increased exponentially tonight. You really are good at your job."

Her stomach did that flipping thing again. "Thanks, from you that's a compliment."

"How about that drink? You look like you could use one."

She drew her lip between her teeth, contemplating the idea.

"C'mon, Rylee, we're not going to cross any lines or do anything you don't want to. You already have an idea what I'd like to do but never mind me. It's not unethical to have friends, even if they are cops."

He did look rather appealing in his tight blue jeans and red T-shirt stretched across his sculpted chest. The police gear he wore daily hid his physique. And he was right, she was allowed to have friends, especially since the friends she thought she had were disappointing her. She could use a drink.

"One drink, as friends. Are you okay with *Smitty's*? I go there a lot. It's close to my apartment."

"Never been but I'll follow you."

As usual, *Smitty's* was busy but, it was a weeknight and they found a table by the stage.

Nick drew out a chair for her and sat beside her. "So, this is your hangout?"

"I guess you could call it that. My apartment is two blocks away so I can walk here. The food is pretty good and I rarely cook for myself. I'm comfortable coming alone because I know most of the staff and the bartenders. They probably feel sorry for me, always alone, but they keep an eye on me."

"You're not dating anyone?"

Heat crept up her cheeks. "No."

"So, if I behave myself tonight, there's a chance I can meet you here again?" He waggled his eyebrows and she swatted his arm playfully.

"Stop! You can usually find me here."

Over beers and chili cheese fries, they talked about their favorite places to go and things to do, tried to one-up each other with screw-ups they'd made on various assignments, and sang along with the country band. Her face hurt from laughing. Neither asked the other about cases they were working on or stories they were chasing. Nick walked her to her car shortly before one o'clock.

"This was nice, sweetheart. Can we do it again?"

Before she could answer he cupped her chin and kissed her on the mouth, a soft, tender, salty kiss. "Say yes." He kissed her again and her stomach performed a triple axel.

"Yes."

8

Steel Chaney gently placed the mocha latte in Bentley's outstretched hand. "Here's your sugar overload for the day. Careful, it's hot."

"C'mon, it beats the mud brewed in the break room. It's my two-hundred-and-thirty-calorie extravagance for the day. I'll go for a run tonight."

He eyed her. A few extra pounds wouldn't hurt her. Women today didn't understand that men like curves. Bony ribs were not a turn on. Not that he was looking at his partner in any other way than professionally but he liked Bentley and wanted her to be happy. She was a good police partner. She'd make an outstanding life partner.

"So where are we?" he asked.

The breath she exhaled lifted her bangs off her forehead. "Nowheresville. The carpet wrapped around her is cheap and ordinary, available in any number of stores and online. No strange DNA left, not even a hair, human or otherwise. The phone company finally got back to me with her records. The last tower it pinged is near the Sharpei home but her killer obviously took her purse and phone. Now it's turned off.

"Tomorrow will be a week since we found Jane Doe and everywhere we look is a dead end. How the hell can no one miss the woman? She wasn't some homeless stray." She leaned back in her chair as if deflated.

"The street camera footage came in. I took your suggestion and turned it over to IT. They're processing it but couldn't say how long it would take."

She dabbed her bleeding cuticle with a tissue. "I released Jane Doe's description to the patrol units, what meager details we know—height, weight, approximate age—but that's little for them to go on. In case they learn of a missing person, she'll be on their radar. Maybe."

Chaney nodded. "Good thinking. What about Sharpei?"

"Not much better." Bentley awakened her iPad. "If he had a cell phone, it's turned off. Last location is his home. Poor Dickey has a posse of friends who must be deaf, dumb, and blind. They don't know nothin', and that's a quote from most of them.

"Tommy Walker, aka Tommy the Thumb because he chopped off half of his left thumb while trying to skin a rat at the age of eight, said he hasn't seen Dickey for days and didn't know anything about anything. Same with Angel Molino although he was helpful in telling me that Dickey has been bragging about coming into big money for a job he was going to do. No idea what kind of job or when. Doesn't sound on the up and up to me, and Angel couldn't or wouldn't provide more details. He also mentioned *The Last Sip Saloon* as Dickey's primary hangout, which we already knew. That's where I'll find Hector Santiago, who apparently works there. He must not have been there the night someone tossed Dickey with the trash. We didn't interview him and neither did Sergeant Cubb. Whoever Squirrel is, he remains a mystery."

The sigh he released was audible. "I finally got hold of his parents this morning."

Bentley sat up. "You did? Where have they been? Why didn't you call me?"

He shrugged. "On a whim, I drove past their house and knocked. They said they'd been on a ten-day cruise and had gotten home only hours earlier. They did look a little road weary. They were somewhat put out that I showed up unannounced. They were unaware their son wasn't home. When I told them their son was dead, they didn't act surprised. Neither of them was much help. Both Type A personalities, him focused on his online optics career and her busy with the life of a socialite. Lunches, manicures, spa dates. She barely seemed to remember she had a son. Said their daughter was at some kind of retreat. Sounded cultish.

"I found it odd that neither one of them became emotional talking about him or the fact that he was murdered. The dad's first response to that news was he'd have to clear his calendar for the funeral. It felt like they were relieved to be rid of a burden. Dickey was a loser but I kinda felt bad for him."

Bentley grinned. "Listen to you showing sympathy. Is that compassion I see peeping out from under that hardnosed shell?"

"Christ, I hope not." He reached for his ringing phone, screwing up his face as he looked at Bentley. "Damn, it's Rylee from the news station. I give her credit for working a story but she's annoying." He punched the green accept button. "Hey, Rylee, you're on speaker so don't proposition me. Where ya been? You haven't bothered me for a couple of days."

Her laugh trickled from the phone and he smiled. Another woman he knew professionally and liked. Maybe Bentley was right, he was going soft.

"Hi, Detective, glad to know you missed me. I took off Friday and Saturday to tend to a family emergency. But I'm back now. I'm just touching base with you on the body in the trunk. Any idea who she is yet?"

"Is everything all right with your family?" It was polite to ask and a stall tactic.

"Who knows? My sister left her husband and she needed help. I'm sure it will come back to bite me. This is the second time she's left him, but she always goes back. I hate that she drags me into it but what else can I do? Anyway, you don't need to hear my problems, what about the dead woman. Anything new?"

"Not yet."

"Wow, tomorrow will be a week since you found her. You're going to make me file a one-week-later-and-still no-clues story. Makes us all look bad."

He appreciated her empathy. "You're not kidding."

Bentley sipped her latte, her head canted.

He tried to be preemptive. "Thanks for broadcasting her description on the news. No one has called you with any tips, have they?" Sometimes people did that and, in the past, the news channel had been cooperative in sharing those phone calls.

"No, sorry. After this phone call I'll tweet that the investigation is ongoing and repeat the request for tips. Is there a reward? That always helps. Isn't there anything new you can share with me? Just one little tidbit?"

He imagined her holding up her thumb and forefinger a quarter inch apart. "Um, not really. Nothing new on the Dickeyfront either."

"Yeah, he didn't seem too helpful when I talked to him. I'm still—"

Chaney sat up straight in his chair and Bentley's eyes widened. "When did you talk to Dickey?"

Rylee stopped mid-sentence. "Huh? It was the night he found the dead woman. Last Wednesday. After you guys released him."

"Where? Who was he with?"

Silence prevailed on the other end of the phone. Rylee wasn't stupid. "What's going on, Detective?"

"Where did you meet him, Rylee? Was he alone? It's important that you tell me."

"Why?"

Bentley caught his attention and mouthed 'she doesn't know'. Of course, not if she'd been off for a couple days. Chaney remembered that her family lived just over the Ohio border, about a two-hour drive. She wouldn't have heard the radio chatter when Dickey's body was discovered, and police hadn't publicly released his identity yet. The media knew only that a suspected homeless man was found dead. Where they got the homeless idea, he didn't know and neither he nor Parker had taken any steps to correct that. Rylee was such a fixture at crime scenes, he'd assumed she knew about this one.

"Look, kiddo, there's been a development. Can we talk off the record? Will you answer my questions if I share some information with you that may be key to the dead woman's case? Information that you can't broadcast right now."

Bentley hurriedly scrawled on the back of an envelope, *Is that a good idea?*

He shrugged. Rylee hadn't answered. "Is that a deal?"

"Um, yeah, okay. I'm trusting you not to back me into a corner, Detective. Or give the story to someone else."

Who else? No one was as dogged as her.

"No worries. Off the record?"

"Okay, off the record, at least for now. What's going on?"

"Dickey Sharpei was found murdered Saturday."

Rylee's gasp was loud enough for Bentley to jump.

"Oh my God. How? Where?"

"We found him dead, just like we found Jane Doe. He—"

Her voice was shrill. "You mean he was in the trunk of a car? In somebody's driveway?"

"No, no, no, hold on. I meant he wasn't killed where we

found him. He was dumped in an alley, dumped like Jane Doe. Your station reported a dead homeless man. Don't they update you after you're away?" It should have clicked then, the young man reporting the story instead of Rylee. "When did you talk to him?"

"Holy shit, are you kidding me? Dickey wasn't homeless."

"Yeah, we're not sure how that became part of the narrative. What can you tell me? Where did you see him?"

Her voice was uneven. "I, um, I saw him at a bar the night of Jane Doe. I tried to talk to him, but his buddies are jagoffs and kept harassing me, and he didn't really tell me anything. Then I went to his house the next day, but no one was home. After I got back from the trip from hell, I looked for him at his hangout. His crew was there but not him and they weren't very cooperative about where he might be. Detective, do you think Jane Doe and Dickey are connected?"

How had she known Sharpei's hangout when he and Bentley just learned it?

"Well, if they aren't it's a hell of a fluke. Let's back up. Where did you see him the first time?"

"At *Smitty's*. It's kind of a neighborhood dive but I know the bartenders and bouncers so I'm comfortable eating or drinking by myself. It's close to my apartment. Seeing Dickey that night surprised me. I'd never seen him there before and neither had the bartender."

"Do you know the bartender's name?"

"Yeah, Elliott."

He was jotting notes on a legal pad. Bentley typed on her iPad. "Elliott what?"

Her laugh sounded more like a giggle. "Elliott with the beautiful blue eyes. I have no idea what his last name is but he's there most nights. Send Parker in, she'll pick him out right away."

Bentley smiled and tapped her iPad screen. He rolled his

eyes. Some lead this would be. "Okay, so you saw Dickey there and then what?"

"I tried to talk to him but he didn't give me any information. Said he had a good lawyer and that's why he was out with his friends. He admitted that he was scared to death when he found her. I politely declined to point out that was obvious by the front of his pants."

He chuckled. Her humor was as twisted as Bentley's.

"Elliott told me he was a regular at *The Last Sip Saloon* and I tried to find him there. But only his buddies were there."

Bentley leaned toward his phone. "You went to *The Last Sip*? Are you crazy? Did you have a camera crew with you? You didn't go alone, I hope."

"No camera but I, um, I had a friend with me. If you want to find his gang of scumbags, that's where you should look. Okay, I've given you my information, give me something. And not just a crumb."

Chaney leaned forward as well, as if the phone wouldn't pick up his voice from his desk chair. "Honestly, these two cases have us stumped. I can tell you that both victims weren't killed where their bodies were discovered. Dickey was shot once between the eyes."

"Where was he found?"

They hadn't released that information yet but Rylee was giving them a solid connection between *The Last Sip Saloon* and Sharpei. He looked at Bentley, silently asking her approval, and she nodded. "He was found behind the dumpster at *The Last Sip Saloon*. No one else has the location so there's your scoop. Do not use his name yet. And stop saying he was homeless."

"Holy shit. He went back there to get high. Maybe it was an accident."

How did she know all this? "How do you know that?"

"His buddies tried to get me to go out back. Said Dickey

might be back there smoking a joint. I didn't buy it though. Jesus, what if I'd gone out there with them?"

"You'd probably be a rape case I'd have to work," Bentley said. "Glad you were smart enough not to believe them. Did they indicate when they last saw Dickey or where he might be? Do you know who any of them are?"

Chaney scratched his head. Had they been there that night among the crowd of gawkers? Patrol units collected the names of the witnesses. He muted his phone. "We had a list of witnesses that night. Where is it?" Bentley rapidly scrolled through her notes.

"I don't know their names," Rylee said. "They were just dicking with me and enjoying it. It takes a big man to bully a woman, you know. They were primates."

Chaney unmuted and laughed at that. "No doubt. It sounds like you handled yourself okay. But do me a favor, stay away from that place for now. Not because it's where we found Dickey. It's a crap heap and not safe for a girl like you."

"Aw, thanks, Detective. Don't worry. You don't have to say it twice. One more thing, am I accurate if I report that Jane Doe and the so far unidentified shooting victim were both killed and dumped, leaving few clues for investigators?"

"I don't like that but yeah, it's accurate." Might as well make her look good for her bosses. At least somebody would look good because it sure wasn't him or Parker.

"Thanks. I'll check back later to see if there are any more developments."

Less than ten minutes passed before Bentley read the headline from the news station's website. True to her word, Rylee didn't identify the victim, and she discounted the idea that he was homeless, instead giving his age and saying he was a suburban resident whose name police were withholding for the time being. She tweeted that foul play was involved, identified the location where the body was found and drew the parallel with Jane Doe.

"That's a little more than I told her," Chaney grumbled.

"You didn't expect her to follow your script, did you? She's not stupid. She probably has the police report from Jane Doe's discovery, which identifies twenty-five-year-old Richard Sharpei as the witness, plus she was at the scene so she knows where he lives. She only used the facts that she knows as well as what you fed her. She didn't violate your confidence."

He studied Bentley. "That's the second time you defend her. How come?"

"I'm not defending her. I'm teaching you to watch what you say around her. She's no one's puppet."

Two hours later, they both appreciated how ambitious she was. Rylee interviewed Mrs. Sharpei, who confirmed on camera the murdered man was her son. She demanded police accountability for Dickey, whom she claimed was a key witness in an ongoing investigation and should have been under police protection. Chaney cursed out loud after she promised a lawsuit. "Laquisha's gonna love this."

AFTER HANGING up with Detective Chaney, Rylee dropped her face into her hands and took calming breaths. Dickey Sharpei was murdered. Maybe not long after she spoke with him. Did one of his ape friends do it? Did they know who did?

She trembled as the thoughts rumbled through her brain like an earthquake's aftershock. She scrolled through her contacts to locate Nick Cooper's number, grateful now that he'd logged it in her phone. If he was working, she'd leave a message. She needed someone to talk to.

"Hey, Rylee, what's up?"

Her heart jumped. "Hi, I wasn't sure if you were on duty. I—"

"I am on duty. I'm on patrol. But you never call so I figured it must be important."

Tears welled in her eyes, surprising her. Was it the news of Dickey's death that unnerved her or that she mattered to Nick? "Oh, sorry to bother you. I, um, I just…"

"What's the matter?"

"I need a friend."

"You dialed the right number. What happened?"

"Remember that guy I was trying to find at the bar? Dickey Sharpei? He's dead."

Astonishment laced Nick's voice. "Dead? How? When?"

"He was shot in the forehead, maybe sometime after I talked to him." She couldn't control the tremor in her voice. "I just found out. The detectives don't have a timeframe yet. But they found his body behind *The Last Sip Saloon*. Do you think his friends knew he was dead when I was asking about him?"

Nick's breath filled her ear. "Anything's possible. Are you all right?"

"I guess so. Is there any chance you don't have plans tonight and could meet me for a drink?"

"Absolutely. I'm off at three unless all hell breaks loose."

She smiled. "I'll be at the station until about six unless all hell breaks loose. Do you mind *Smitty's* again?"

"I'll be there."

She disconnected the call feeling somewhat better. Nick was easy to talk to and he'd understand her concerns about Jane Doe's murder and Dickey's connection. Dickey's words—that he'd fucked up—puzzled her. What was he supposed to do with Jane Doe's car and with her? And who expected it?

Nick seemed trustworthy and, unlike Tessa, Nick understood her need to dissect the details and make sense of them. She could never play 'what if' with Tessa. Rylee could discuss both murders and possible stories with Nick without being ridiculed or dismissed as obsessive. Tessa would do both. She patted herself on the back for calling her new friend.

Her phone rang with a blocked number minutes after she hung up from Nick. "This is Janet Sharpei. I found your business card tucked in the front door."

Rylee bolted out of her chair, grabbed a fresh notebook, and plopped back down. "Yes, ma'am." When she left the card, her goal was to talk to Dickey and learn more about the night he found Jane Doe. This interview would be much different now.

Mrs. Sharpei opened the conversation with a volley of insults aimed at Rylee for her insensitivity and intrusion on the family's grief. It took several minutes to calm her down and explain that she'd left the card almost a week earlier, before her son was killed.

"You have my deepest sympathy, Mrs. Sharpei. I knew Dickey a little, I spoke to him shortly before..." Her words were met with silence. "He seemed a little, um, aimless maybe. Would you like to talk to me about him? I'd welcome an interview with you and your husband." She flipped the reason for her call to a chance for Mrs. Sharpei to give testimony about her son's life as well as plead for any witnesses to come forward to help solve the crime. A half hour later, she sat at the Sharpei's kitchen table, cameras rolling. Mark Sharpei was out of town on business, she said. That puzzled Rylee. So soon after his son's death?

The house was so clean it was almost impersonal. She'd bet a professional service kept it that way. She hadn't noticed any family photos on the way from the front door to the back kitchen. White walls everywhere. Abstract artwork that was probably expensive. The place felt more like a museum than a home.

Janet Sharpei portrayed her son as a lost soul, not cut out for college and unlucky in the handful of career paths that he'd chosen, still coming of age and finding himself. The productive life that lay before him had been heinously cut short by a bullet, she said with more anger than loss in her voice. She didn't cry for her son. Her tone wasn't even mournful. Rylee sensed there was more the woman could say.

"Do you know about the incident with the strange car being left in your driveway? Did Dickey talk to you about that?"

She lit a cigarette. "We were out of town. He said the police were here. All he told me was that he'd lost a bet. It was some ridiculous social media dare to find someone else's car at your home and relocate it without getting caught or something like that. I guess all the kids are doing it now." Rylee felt her eyebrows knit. Was there video of the event? She hadn't heard of a challenge like that.

"It is?"

Mrs. Sharpei sighed. "Dickey said it was. They leave the key hidden somewhere and someone else finds it and drives the car away. It doesn't make sense to me. Dickey said they tried to prank him but he didn't go along with the joke because he thought it might get him in trouble. He doesn't drive." She inspected her fresh manicure. "He ran afoul of the law once before, but you probably know that. He was trying to straighten out his life."

Rylee gulped. "Did he say who left the car for him?" She held her breath.

"No. And I didn't ask. It sounded childish and I told him so."

"But he told you it was a game of sorts?"

"I guess, yes."

"Did he tell you what was inside the car?"

"No. It was a terrible connection when we spoke. We were on a cruise and didn't talk long. I only called to inquire about a package I was expecting. I told him to grow up and stop playing juvenile games."

Rylee interrupted. "A package? May I ask what was in it? Could it have something to do wi-with," she stuttered, "with what happened?"

Janet Sharpei rolled her eyes. "I highly doubt new swimsuits for me had anything to do with my son's murder."

"I'm sorry. Did he say anything else about the car?"

"He said someone else had something to do with it but I'm not clear on the details. It doesn't matter. The police came and didn't believe him. And now he's dead."

She turned to the camera. "It's important to stress that the police knew my son was a witness to whatever happened here and they failed to protect him. We're considering a civil suit."

Rylee was dumbfounded. No wonder Dickey was a loose cannon. No parental guidance. She motioned for the cameraman to cut the interview off.

"I'd like to attend the funeral if you wouldn't mind, Mrs. Sharpei, just to pay my respects. I won't bring a camera crew with me but, with your permission, I'll report it."

"You're welcome to come. You can film if you like. I'm sure there will be a huge turnout. My husband and I are well connected." No mention of Dickey's friends.

Rylee edited the tape in the camera van, leaving out the details Janet Sharpei thought she knew about the abandoned car and that the sole reason she spoke to her dead son was to check on a swimsuit delivery. The focus of this broadcast was Dickey's murder. She filmed her report standing in the Sharpei's driveway. It was the lead story on all the news time slots.

9

The day had been exhilarating and exhausting. Rylee drove into *Smitty's* parking lot feeling drained and immediately smiled when she saw Nick leaning against a black Harley, motorcycle helmet in hand.

He waited at her driver's door, opening it once the ignition switched off and the locks unlocked. She stepped out. He cupped her chin and dropped a soft kiss on her lips. "I saw your newscast. You kicked ass."

Her heart fluttered from the touch of his lips and his compliment. "Thanks." She nodded toward the helmet. "I didn't know you had a motorcycle. It's beautiful."

He laid his hand between her shoulder blades as they walked toward the door. "Thanks. How about I take you for a ride on Sunday? Maybe up to Moraine State Park for a picnic? I won't have another weekend day off for a couple weeks so it's kind of now or never. We don't have much summer left."

"Okay." The word slipped out before she could catch herself. But she liked the idea.

Nick guided her to an empty table, grinning. Well why not? Like he said, she was allowed to have friends and he seemed to be the only one showing up for her. Still radio silence from Tessa.

Once they ordered drinks and food, she stretched her right hand to grasp his left. "Can I talk to you about something? Not as a policeman but I want to pick your cop brain. Just between me and you?"

His thumb rolled over the top of her hand. "Sure. My brain is all yours."

"Dickey said something that's been bothering me. I don't know what to make of it but a voice in my head tells me there's substance to it." She filled her lungs. His words had haunted her.

"When I was talking to him the first time here," she nodded to the corner of the bar where they'd stood, "well, the only time I talked to him, he said he fucked up. He said he didn't do what he was supposed to do. He—"

"What does that mean, 'what he was supposed to do.' About what?"

"When he found the body in the car. Jane Doe. He said the minute he saw the car, he knew it was bad. And he wasn't supposed to call the police."

She had Nick's full attention. "What was he supposed to do?"

"That's what I don't know. He said it was big shit and that there had been talk about what to do if he found himself in that situation." She tilted her head to one side. "Who the hell talks about what to do if you find a dead body in your driveway?"

Nick sipped his beer, his eyes narrowed. "Someone who's planning a murder and wants you as an accomplice."

"That thought crossed my mind but Dickey? An unreliable pothead? He pissed himself when he found her. That's not the reaction you have if you're expecting it."

"Did he say anything else?"

"Just that he wasn't taking the rap for it. He didn't do what he was supposed to do but he," she withdrew her hand from his and made air quotes, "ain't goin' down for this."

The waiter deposited their dinner plates and Rylee dug into her steak salad. She pointed with her fork. "He was part of something, I'm sure, some plan to kill that woman and dispose of her body. And he got cold feet. And that's why he's dead now."

Nick nodded. "Sounds plausible. But a plan with who? None of his friends looked capable of planning their next meal, let alone a murder. And Jane Doe was well-to-do, not some street worker or homeless person. It's unlikely she ran in Dickey's crowd."

Rylee stared at him. "How do you know that?"

Nick's eyebrows rose. "After we went to the saloon and you said he was connected to the Jane Doe in the trunk, I looked up the reports. I was pretty sure you weren't going to let it go and I wanted to know what you were getting into."

"What'd the report say?"

Nick lowered his fork and sat back. "That's not how this relationship is going to work, Rylee. I'd like to be part of your life but I won't be a source."

The corners of her mouth dipped. "You're right. I'm sorry. I shouldn't have asked that and I won't ever do that again. It's just—"

"There is no 'just', about this. It has to be a hard and fast rule."

Her face heated. "I'm sorry. It will be. It is. What I was going to say is it's just exciting to talk about my work with someone who understands. I couldn't wait to talk to you. And my natural inclination to ask questions got the better of me. That said, I plan to attend Dickey's funeral. Is it against the rules to ask if you will come with me?"

She frowned. "That didn't sound right. I'm not asking you

out to a funeral. I'm hoping my handy dandy backup is available again."

The right side of Nick's mouth curved up. "Are you wondering if the killer will show up to admire his work?"

She nodded.

"Are you sure you weren't a cop in another life? That's exactly what I would do. Let me know when it is and I'll try to change my schedule. If I can't, I've got a buddy I trust who can be your backup."

ONE WEEK and one day after Jane Doe's body was discovered and five days after Dickey Sharpei was found murdered, Rylee and Nick walked through the crowded parking lot and into the funeral home. As it turned out, she wasn't the only one curious about who might attend Dickey Sharpei's final soiree. Parker Bentley stood against the back wall at the funeral home, opposite the front doors, making note of everyone who entered. She nodded at Rylee and Rylee acknowledged her the same way.

Inside the viewing room, Steel Chaney assumed a similar position in a far corner. Rylee looked briefly at Dickey. They'd dressed him in a faded T-shirt and leather jacket. A dirty ballcap drawn low over his closed eyes concealed the fatal wound. Nick grasped her elbow and guided her toward the back of the room. Chaney surprised her by smiling.

"Hey, Cuz." Chaney extended his hand to Nick who shook it and then embraced him. "What are you doing here?"

Nick drew her closer. "I'm backup. Rylee's on the trail of a hot news story."

Chaney's grin grew wider. "When isn't she?" He tsked at her. "You should be careful about the company you keep. I thought you were smarter than this." He jabbed Nick's shoulder.

She'd never seen Chaney act so normal. "Hi, Detective. Are you two related?" Why hadn't Nick mentioned it?

A commotion at the front of the room didn't allow time for a response. Nick coaxed her closer to his side as Dickey's friends stumbled in, beer cans in hand. Five of them stood in front of the casket, drinks raised in a salute. They drained the contents and dropped the empties on top of their friend. The Sharpeis were too horrified to stop them.

Ape Number One released a loud yowl, like a hyena, then screamed Dickey's name in one long monotone. "Dickeee-eee-eee." The others repeated it before four men in dark suits approached them and ushered them out. It seemed a fitting send off for their pal.

"I'll be right back." Rylee rushed out of the room, ignoring Nick's plea for her to wait. She chased the group outside, yelling after them. "Wait. Please wait one minute."

Two of them turned to see who called after them. She recognized Sour Breath and Ape Number One with the neck tattoo. Breathless, Rylee ran to them and grabbed Sour Breath's arm.

"What happened to Dickey? I know you know something. Tell me so I can get justice for his murder." The five of them circled around her.

She swallowed her trepidation after Nick called her name and she heard his footfalls on the asphalt behind her. He was her backup. She leveled her gaze on Sour Breath. "Who shot him? He was afraid of someone. One of you knows who killed him, I'd bet my paycheck on it. Tell me so I can help. You were supposed to be his friends."

That struck a nerve. "We are his friends. We tried to help him," Sour Breath snapped. "Dickey was one of us."

"Do you know what happened?"

"I tell you anything, I'm a dead man. Just like Dickey."

"What do you mean? You can trust me. I won't tell."

Ape Number One nudged his shoulder and nodded at something behind her. Parker Bentley was approaching. "This ain't the place. We gotta go."

Rylee yanked her business card holder from the front pocket of her tote. She shoved two cards into Sour Breath's hand. "Please. I want to talk to you some more. Where can I meet you?"

They scattered through the parking lot without looking back. She moved out of the way of three incoming cars and turned when Nick grabbed her elbow.

"Are you crazy? What the hell were you thinking?"

"I wanted to ask them some questions. It's a public parking lot, what could happen? I'm fine."

"A lot can happen out here." Only then did she see the concern on Nick's face. "Please don't do that again."

She touched his cheek. "Sorry. I kind of forgot I wasn't here by myself."

Parker reached them. "Where are they going?" Her tone was brusque and it immediately put Rylee on the defensive.

"How would I know?"

Parker glared at her. "What'd they say?"

She reached for Nick's hand. "Nothing. Come on, let's go back in."

Parker turned dismissively, her spine stiff, and strode toward the building ahead of them.

Rylee eyed the mourners just arriving and stopped walking. Nick looked at her with an unasked question on his lips. Peter Owens stepped out of a sleek, silver racecar he'd driven into a handicapped parking space. At least it looked like a racecar with doors that glided upward like a bird's wing instead of swinging out to the side. What was he doing here? He popped a mint in his mouth, pocketed the tin and took the steps two at a time.

She and Nick followed a group of three through the front

door. She didn't see Owens anywhere. Nick led her to stand beside Detective Chaney again just as Owens entered the viewing room.

Did he know the Sharpeis? Mrs. Sharpei had described them as well connected. Did she mean politically?

Peter Owens wore a dark gray suit with a light gray shirt and a black tie. He approached Mrs. Sharpei first, clasping her hand in his and whispering words Rylee couldn't hear. He kissed her on each cheek and turned to Mr. Sharpei. The men hugged. He adjusted his perfectly knotted tie as he pivoted toward the room.

She laid her hand on Nick's chest. "I'm going out to the other room. I want to ask him about Tessa." She walked away before he could object.

She waited for Owens in the reception room where Parker was back on watch. Peter Owens hugged the women and shook hands with the men on the path to the exit. Her nose crinkled. That was a little forward, wasn't it? As he came through the doorway, he discreetly removed a travel-sized bottle of hand sanitizer from his jacket pocket and dabbed his palms. It disappeared quickly when he noticed Rylee watching him.

He assumed the grin she associated with The Joker and opened his arms. "Rylee, what a surprise." She stepped backward to avoid his hug.

"Hello Mr. Owens. I'm surprised to see you here as well. Do you know the Sharpeis?"

His grin widened showing all thirty-two artificially whitened teeth. "Mr. Owens? Is my father here?" He looked to either side, affecting a laugh that sounded more like a growl.

Rylee grinned, keeping her lips tight. "Are you friends with the Sharpeis?"

His eyes widened. "Uh, no, not exactly. But this is such a tragic accident, my heart went out to the family and I decided to pay my respects."

Accident? Dickey was murdered.

Nick stepped into her line of vision, watching but not intruding. Her shoulders relaxed.

"That was nice of you. I haven't been able to reach Tessa. Do you know where she's been?"

She declined the breath mint he offered. "Uh no, not really. She mentioned that you two had a spat. You know she's flighty sometimes." He patted her shoulder. "I wouldn't worry about it."

Her eyebrows drew close. A spat? Because she wanted to talk to Dickey when they were at *Smitty's*? That couldn't be the issue. "Well, please tell her I'm trying to reach her. Did you find out anything about her car? Did Mrs. Owens contact you?"

The grin returned. "I'm not sure what you're talking about, honey. You know me and Mrs. Owens aren't on speaking terms. It was good to see you." He patted her shoulder again and walked toward another man near the door. He ignored her when she called after him.

Nick still watched her from the archway. She walked to him and whispered, "I've never liked talking to that man but that was just odd. He acted like he didn't know anything about Tessa's car being dragged out of the river. I have so many questions." Nick stood a foot taller than her so she looked up to his gaze. "I'm not saying that as a reporter. I'm saying that as your... um..." She gulped.

Nick dropped his hand on her shoulder and his thumb caressed the back of her neck. "However you finish that sentence is fine with me. Do you want to stay longer? I switched with Parsons, who's on midnights, so I work tonight. If we leave now, we can grab a bite to eat. I don't have my uniform with me so I have to run to my place before I get to the station by ten-thirty. If you want to stay longer, Steel will give you a ride home."

"You didn't tell me you are related."

His right eyebrow arched. "We haven't spent enough time together to talk about our families. How many cousins do you have that I don't know about?"

Well, he had a point. "You're right. Sorry. We can leave now. I've seen enough. Thanks for changing your schedule for me."

"Any time. Remember, we have a date on Sunday."

She posted a respectful item about Dickey's service, leaving out Peter Owens and, after much deliberation, including "a unique tribute from Mr. Sharpei's closest friends."

10

Sunday morning, Rylee was ready by nine o'clock. Hearing the roar of the Harley come down her street, she swallowed her nerves. She'd never ridden a motorcycle before but Nick's guarantees over the phone calmed her. They'd talked every day since that first night at *Smitty's*. Their conversations sometimes lasted an hour when they shared the highlights of their days or complained about them. Her heart flipped every time she saw his name on the phone screen.

She waited for him to climb the fire escape and, as always, was slightly embarrassed by her apartment when she motioned him in the open door. It had once been a single-family home that was converted into three apartments. Her second-floor unit used to be three bedrooms on one floor but now was a bedroom, a kitchen with a small bathroom built in the corner to optimize the proximity of the kitchen plumbing, and a larger room she used as a living, dining, ironing, craft, and anything else room. The carpet was cheap, the blinds practically transparent and the appliances secondhand. But it was spotless.

Above her was an even smaller efficiency apartment just as outdated. The homeowner had turned the side windows into doors and erected a fire escape along the wall of the house so she and the upstairs tenant had private entrances. In winter, the metal steps were slippy. She'd added her own chain lock to the door two days after moving in and finding a man peering in the window, supposedly looking for the former occupant.

Nick looked around. "This is nice."

She shut the door behind him. "It's a dump. My furniture is mostly from donation centers. You know, one man's trash is a struggling reporter's treasure. The pipes bang when someone uses hot water for any length of time and I hear what's going on above and below me. But it's affordable. Thanks for being kind enough to lie."

One long stride moved him farther into the room and positioned him beside the sofa. "I thought you TV types made the big bucks. I planned on dating you for your money."

He had such a knack for making her relax. She laughed.

"You have an intoxicating laugh, do you know that?"

Drunk was how she felt around him. Damn if he didn't look good in leather. "Only the anchors on the desk, the so-called faces of Channel 5, are paid well. Us grunts survive on the low end of livable compensation. The communications business is notoriously cheap. Sorry to disappoint you."

He winked, sending a trill down her spine. "Nothing about you disappoints me. Are you ready?"

Per his instructions, she wore blue jeans, tennis shoes, and a long-sleeved, lightweight T-shirt. "I just want to tie my hair back."

"Do you have a change of clothes in a bag somewhere? A purse?" He extended a backpack toward her. "Will they fit in here?"

"Sure, but I have a backpack."

"This has a sternum strap. It will give you better balance and stay on in case we wipe out."

Her mouth dropped open but she relaxed when he grinned. "We won't, but I'd rather you use this."

She transferred the contents of her crossbody purse and travel backpack with room to spare. Two bottles of water fit handily in the mesh side pockets. She eyed the other items in his hand. "What else?"

He used his index finger to motion her toward him and when she was close, he squatted in front of her. "Step into these."

"What are they?" She balanced on his shoulder and slipped one leg in the leather pant leg and then the other.

"Chaps. Turn around please."

Nick closed four snaps on the side of each leg, rolling up the extra length at her ankles. "These are a little big for you." He deftly laced the backs of her thighs and cinched the waist. "It's not perfect but it's good enough." He stood.

Rylee ran her hand down the soft leather. "I feel like a biker babe. Did these, um, did they belong to a former girlfriend?"

She regretted the comment when Nick cupped her chin and kissed her, the longest kiss he'd delivered so far. Soft and minty. She returned the kiss, sorry that it ended so quickly.

"You're not the first woman I've taken on the bike. But you're the first one I've cared enough about to protect. Thanks for being a little jealous."

"That sounds mean."

"I don't mean it like that. The street clothes you have on would be fine. With you, I'm going the extra mile. Here, slip into this." He lifted a leather jacket from the couch and held it open for her to slide in her arms. "I borrowed these from Mona. You'll meet her today."

"It's not going to be just us?" She was somewhat disappointed and a little relieved. This guy was making her feel things.

He readjusted the jacket. "I like the sound of that, you know.

We have a regular group who meet at the park. Today is our last hurrah for the summer. Everyone pitches in and Mona coordinates a lunch of sorts. Nothing fancy. It will be fun but yeah, we can make time for just us if you want. Got everything?"

She followed him down the fire escape and listened attentively while he coached her not to put her feet down, not to lean into the curve and not to let go of him until she was comfortable. "You don't have to let go at all," he said nonchalantly as he tightened the strap on her helmet, then adjusted the backpack on her shoulders. "I'd prefer that."

She imagined the entire neighborhood running to their windows when he fired up the engine, straddled the Harley and she climbed on behind him. Okay, it felt damn good wrapping her arms around his waist.

Driving out of the city was tedious but once they were on the highway, exhilaration claimed her. "Nick, this is a feeling I can't describe. It's like freedom."

"I hoped you'd like it." His voice sounded gravely through the helmet microphone. "I love riding this thing."

The closer they got to the state park, the fresher the air. By the time he parked beside more than two dozen various motorcycles, she felt giddy. He unhooked her helmet. When he knelt to undo the chaps, her body went on full alert with his hands on her. He removed a blanket from the saddlebag on the bike, rolled the chaps into the empty space, took her hand, and started up a path. In the distance, rock music blared from a pavilion.

Two couples sat at a table and waved. "Hey, Coop." Nick nodded. "How much did you pay her to come with you today?"

Next to them at another table, three women and two men howled at the comment. "When you discover how boring he is, honey, come sit with us," one of the men yelled.

Nick blushed.

"Are these your friends?"

"You'd never know it. Do you prefer sun or shade?"

"Either. Whatever you like."

He stopped about thirty feet from the pavilion and spread out the blanket. "Bathrooms are over there if you want to change. They're pretty clean." He dropped the helmets on a corner of the blanket and eased the leather jacket off her shoulders. "If you want something to eat or drink now, we can check out the spread."

"No, I'm fine. I'll change." She'd debated what to wear and opted for shorts and a halter top with built in support. She didn't need much in that area anyway. She was lucky to have a high metabolism that, for now, kept her slim. But after passing some of the other women on her way back to the blanket, she decided her arms were flabby. Maybe Nick could help her tone up. He looked like he worked out.

He lay on the blanket, his eyes closed and his face to the sun when she returned. He'd removed his shirt and wore a powder blue tank that stretched across flat abs. Oh yeah, he worked out. The tribal tattoo on his left shoulder surprised her. Dark hairy legs poked out of navy gym shorts that stopped at his knees. He'd kicked off his boots and socks and she admired his bare feet. How a man cares for his feet is telling. His nails were trimmed and his heels looked smooth.

The second he sensed her there, he sat up, smiled, and offered his hand. She took it and sat down beside him. He positioned the backpack behind her and she lay back, using it as a pillow.

She closed her eyes and the prior week's tensions melted in the warm sun.

"All good?"

"Mmmm, this is heaven."

He stretched out beside her, his hands behind his head. "This is better than any therapist's couch. I always find balance after a day on the bike."

"I'm envious. Everything stays in my head and rolls around all the time."

"You want to talk about it? I'm a good listener."

She already knew that. "I don't know. My emotions are all over the place about my friend, Tessa. I'm worried about her. She's not returning my calls. And that makes me angry with her and it conflicts me. It feels like something is wrong. Like badly wrong. I was scared to death when you were dragging her car out of the river. I thought she might have committed suicide or worse."

Her eyes remained closed but Nick's breath on her cheek told her he'd turned to look at her. "Worse? Like what?"

"Like maybe she found her mother and they had a terrible fight and something bad happened to Tessa. It sounds ridiculous, I know."

"Not so ridiculous. You care about your friend and you're worried. I get it. What else?"

She grinned. He was starting to know her too well. "The whole Dickey murder. It doesn't make sense. I feel like his friends expect me to figure it out. I—"

"That's a job for the police, honey. They'll solve it."

"I know, I know. It's just weighing on me. Let's not talk about me. I'm seeking balance. Tell me something to make me smile." She glanced at him but his face was to the sun again. In profile his nose was straight. Just a hint of a beard. No shaving on his day off.

"Okay. You won't believe me, though. I've thought about bringing you here since the first day I met you."

She stared at him but his eyes stayed closed. "I don't remember the first time we met."

"You were reporting the Norton trial. It was before I transferred downtown."

"I don't remember you. Did you testify?"

"No, they never called me. But you ran after Sergeant

Schultz down the hall and he introduced us. You blew me off because I wasn't a witness and couldn't tell you anything. I started watching the news after that."

"You make me sound awful. That was more than a year ago, wasn't it?"

"Yep."

"And you remember me from that? Come on, be serious."

He finally looked at her. "I am. And yeah, I do. I knew then I wanted you in my life."

She giggled. "Oh yeah, right. How'd you know that?"

He rolled over to cover half her body with his. A shiver of anticipation ran along her side where they touched. "When you know, you know, Rylee." His kiss was passionate, designed to turn her on and it did the job. His tongue grazed her lips, her teeth, and her tongue. She drank every incredible feeling in, moaning when his hand on her hip nudged her closer.

"Get a room, you two," someone yelled to the delight of everyone. Nick dropped one final kiss on her mouth and sat up. "Sorry about that."

Sorry? What was he sorry about? Her head spun. Her heart soared.

"We better go up to the pavilion before I ruin your reputation and break a couple laws." He stood and helped her up, holding her hand while they walked to the group.

"Everyone, this is Rylee." Politely, they ignored the color she was certain reddened her face. One by one, he rattled off their names identifying most of them as cops from other departments or zones. The men nodded, the women smiled. If they recognized her, no one said anything.

This was why she shouldn't get involved with Nick. What if tomorrow, she was assigned a story that required her to show up at one of these officer's stations? She asked that question on the drive home, clinging to Nick even more tightly.

It had been a marvelous day. They'd played volleyball in a

group and she surprised Nick with her skill. She'd played competitive sports in college. They ate, drank pop and lemonade because none of them drank alcohol when riding their bikes, and joked a lot. They spent more time beside each other on the blanket too but Nick kept the PDA in check. Everyone said they hoped to see her at another riders' function with him. She hoped so too.

"Knowing them outside of the police station doesn't change anything. If they are allowed to give you information, they will. If not, they'll tell you who to talk to. I don't want to insult you, honey, but you're not that big a deal. You're good at your job, you get your stories and you report them fairly. No one resents that. Just because you were at a picnic today doesn't mean Simon or Ramsey will hide from you tomorrow or see you and tell you things they shouldn't. We all have a job to do."

He turned off the ignition, helped her off the motorcycle and followed her up the stairs. "Did you have a good time today?"

She did. Opening the door, he followed her inside and took her in his arms when she turned. "I really did. Thank you for taking me with you."

Anything else she planned to say was stifled by his kiss. Possessive. Demanding. Promising.

Reluctantly, he released her and reached for the door. "I wish I could stay." The bulge in his jeans verified that. "I'm on duty tonight. Today was perfect. I was proud to be with you. I want more days like today. Aw, hell, I want more." He yanked her into a tight hug again and took her breath away with one final kiss. "Thanks for making my dream come true. I'll call you later."

She stood staring at the closed door, her body pulsing for more as well. What just happened?

11

Rylee pounded on the Owens' front door early Monday morning. Enough was enough. Tessa couldn't ignore her if she stood on her doorstep. It was just after seven-thirty. Pearl Owens was an early riser and if Tessa had to work today, she'd be up already. If she didn't, the pounding would wake her up. Either way, Rylee was putting an end to this so-called spat.

She wanted her best friend back. And she wanted to talk about Nick and the feelings she was starting to have for him.

She dialed Tessa's cell number, rang the doorbell, and knocked again. The door swung wide and Peter Owens stared at her.

"Rylee? It's a little early for all this commotion, don't you think?"

The surprise at finding him instead of Tessa or Pearl Owens in the doorway, barefoot in a white cotton bathrobe, dropped her jaw. She recovered quickly.

"I'm sorry, Mr. Owens but I'd like to see Tessa. Is she up?"

The joker grinned. "Tessa's not here."

"Oh, did she leave for work already?"

"No, she's not here. She took a spontaneous vacation. She's visiting my sister in Florida."

"Aunt Betty?"

"Yes. Betty hasn't been well and Tessa agreed to be her temporary caretaker."

"Really? When did she decide to do that? What about her job?"

"You know how capricious she can be. Anyway, she hated that job. She couldn't say one thing good about it. Would you like to come in for a cup of coffee?"

Her thoughts spun out of control. Tessa left town without telling her? They'd talked about visiting Aunt Betty together, turning it into a mini vacation. Peter Owens was staying at the house? Where was Pearl?

"Did Mrs. Owens go with her?" She doubted it. According to Tessa, the sisters-in-law hated each other.

"I've no idea what Mrs. Owens is doing. How about that coffee?"

"Um, no, thank you. I have to get to work. Would—"

"Just one cup." He tugged on her upper arm. "I wanted to ask you about the Sharpei funeral. I was going to call you later." His grasp was firmer than she liked, drawing her inside. Call her? He'd never done that.

She knew this house like her own and walked straight to the kitchen. Peter Owens followed.

"Can I make you some breakfast? I'm a pro when it comes to scrambled eggs."

She looked around the kitchen sensing something was different but not finding it. Her mind's eye nagged her but her conscious eye failed to see it. She blinked to refocus when Peter Owens repeated her name and held up a frying pan. "No thanks, I don't eat breakfast. Will you be hearing from Tessa? I'd really like to talk to her."

He poured hot coffee into a mug stenciled World's Greatest Mom. Who bought that?

"Sure, sure, I'll tell her to call you. I was surprised to see you at the funeral home. Are you working on that story? I saw you talking to the detectives. Do the police have any leads?"

Why was he asking her what the police knew when he could probably pick up the phone and call his buddy the chief for a firsthand report? He tightened the belt on his robe and she cringed. Was that a bulge?

"I don't know. The detectives rarely tell me anything. My information comes through the chief or the public information officer. I was there to supplement a forthcoming human-interest series. The station is compiling a piece on violence among teenagers."

"I see." His head bobbed. "Dickey was twenty-five. Hardly a teen. Did you know him? Ever talk to him?"

She raised the cup to her lips, blew the steam away, and sipped. She loved coffee but this brew was weak. This whole situation was off. Her spine felt like a tarantula crawled down it.

"I interviewed his mother. Maybe you saw it on TV. After talking to her, I wanted to pay my respects."

"That was nice of you. Janet told me that you knew her son."

"Who?"

"Janet Sharpei."

Now, the hairs on the back of her neck crawled to attention. "No, she's mistaken. I didn't know him." That wasn't a lie. She didn't really know him.

"Oh, well, maybe I misunderstood. Do you—"

"I'm sorry, Mr. Owens, but I have to get a move on or I'll be late."

He slid a metal tin toward her. "Mint? I find coffee breath offensive."

"No thanks. Please tell Tessa to call me as soon as possible.

It's important to me." She glanced around the kitchen one more time. What was it that was wrong?

"I sure will, sweetie. You know, since I'm here by myself and you live by yourself, maybe we could have dinner together. After all, you're my daughter's best friend. I have to take care of you like you're my own. I could whip up something here if you didn't want to go somewhere."

What. The. Actual. Fuck? Was he living here now? Since when? She headed toward the front door, Owens following behind her like a puppy. A hard yank opened it.

"Thanks, but I'm sort of seeing someone and well, you know how it is, we try to spend all our time together. Tell Tessa to call."

She was on her way down the porch steps. She would have jumped down them if she could to get away that much faster. Where was Pearl Owens?

Once in her car, she checked the time. Nick should be off shift. By now, they knew each other's schedules. Yesterday's picnic had shifted their relationship. She felt closer to him and, if being honest, had imagined last night while lying in bed alone what it might be like to be naked and close.

She dragged her phone from the bottom of her purse, balanced it on her knee while driving and punched the keys to dial his number. Someday, maybe she'd own a car with hands-free capabilities.

"Hey you, good morning."

"Hey, can you talk? How was your night?"

"Not bad at all. A couple car accidents and business alarms. Nothing that would interest you. You sound like you're yelling. Where are you?"

"I'm driving. My phone is in the cup holder. Can you meet me sometime today? I know you have to sleep so whatever time works for you."

"Everything okay?"

"I was just hoping I could talk to you about some stuff. I, um…" She was what? Freaked out by Peter Owens? Concerned about Pearl? Angry about Tessa? Happy that she had someone she could call when she felt like this?

Nick filled the silence. "How about dinner? I'm off the rest of the day. If you want to meet now, I could buy you breakfast."

"Aren't you tired?"

"Not too tired for you."

Her heart leapt. "I'm on my way to work. Dinner sounds good. Six o'clock at *Smitty's*. Go home and get some sleep."

"You get off the phone while you're driving. It's against the law, you know."

His laugh teased her ear even after he hung up. She was probably being paranoid but an older model brown car made the same three turns that she did. As the TV station's parking lot appeared, she breathed a sigh of relief, only to watch the car follow her. The car vibrated from the music that blared, competing with the roar of an exhaust without a muffler. She clutched the pink pepper spray in her right hand when she stepped out of the driver's seat.

The long-haired driver rolled down his window. She recognized him as Sour Breath, one of Dickey's friends from the bar. He took a drag on his cigarette and blew the smoke in her direction. "They done Dickey wrong. Barney Fife ain't gonna give a fuck. Come to the Saloon tonight. Midnight. We'll tell you some things." His tires screeched when he drove away.

THE DAY PASSED QUICKLY. Her editor, Tamara, wisely mixed in a soft news assignment now and then to offset the dark, gritty stories Rylee usually encountered. Rylee often balked at the deviation, but Tamara stood firm. She dispatched her to report a story about an elderly couple who were scammed by a roofing contractor, arguing that a white-collar crime was still a crime. The couple lost their life savings. It broke Rylee's heart.

Before she knew it, she was driving to *Smitty's*, smiling at the idea that Nick would be there. He leaned against his SUV watching her back into a parking space. *Smitty's* lot was small and it was easier to leave if you were already facing out. The later it got, the drunker the drivers. He smiled as she approached him. Geez, she was excited to see him. She walked to him and pressed her arms around his waist, falling against his chest. His arms wrapped around her to draw her closer. His chin rested on the top of her head.

"Hi. You okay?"

Her face remained buried in his muscular pecs. "Shitty day," she mumbled. "I needed this."

He dropped a kiss on her head. "Come home with me and you can spend the night in my arms."

If only. She tightened her embrace. "I can't. I'm meeting Dickey's friends at midnight."

Nick straightened and moved her out to arm's length. "Say again?"

Her shoulders sagged with the weight of the commitment. "Let's get a beer and I'll tell you what happened."

Once they were seated and served, Nick listened to her account of the invitation for tonight. "Your boss is okay with you interviewing someone at midnight in a place like that?"

She took a deep breath. "I didn't tell my editor. This could be a crazy hunch that doesn't pan out and, if I mention something, they'll turn it into a story even if it isn't one. A lot of times they have their own agenda. They go for titillating rather than true. Besides, what could Dickey's baboons know that the police don't?"

"You might be surprised. You're not going alone."

"I was hoping you'd say that."

"I'm not ignoring you, either. We walk in together. You can

go off to the side to get your information but not out of my sight."

She smiled. "I was hoping you'd say that too." The whole encounter with Peter Owens still upset her as she told him about it next.

"I mean, Tessa wouldn't just up and go see Aunt Betty without telling me. We've never gone this long without some kind of communication. I don't get it."

"Maybe she was madder than you thought."

"About a stupid report that her car was dragged from the river? Come on, that's crazy. But what's even crazier is that her father acts like he's back in the Owens home again. Like the king of the roost. Where's Pearl, that's what I want to know. She threw her husband out. Why would she let him waltz back in?"

"He could have paid her a large sum of money to disappear, you know. He has a reputation to preserve and things got ugly during the last election. It's no secret that he has political aspirations and his wife didn't seem like someone who would back down."

"That's just it. Pearl wasn't a woman to back down."

"For the right price, honey, people will do almost anything. You haven't talked to Tessa for days. For all you know, her mother contacted her and they patched things up. Just because you haven't seen her doesn't mean she's not around."

"I guess so." She picked up her phone and punched in Tessa's number. It went straight to voicemail and when Rylee tried to leave a message, the box was full. She frowned. "None of this adds up, Nick. None of it."

He checked his watch. "Well, you can't solve it tonight. It's eight fifteen. We have more than three hours to kill before your midnight rendezvous. Come back to my place. I haven't told you about Quigley. I want you to meet him."

"Who's Quigley?"

SHE FOLLOWED Nick to his home, a small ranch on a busy thoroughfare. He'd told her to park in the garage and he parked behind her car in the narrow, one-car driveway.

"This looks nice," she said as she strolled behind him to a set of wooden steps.

"It's small. I'm already looking for something I like better, something bigger. But this was within the city limits and it was a steal. Caught up in some family estate snafu so I snatched it up. I'm not fond of it though."

"How long have you lived here?"

"Less than a year."

He opened the door at the top of the stairs. Waiting behind it was two-year-old Quigley, his tail wagging so fast it threatened to knock him off balance.

Quigley turned out to be the cutest Beagle Rylee had ever seen.

Nick knelt and the dog lifted up on his back paws to lick his face and accept the loving caresses Nick offered. The heartwarming moment clutched her heart.

Nick looked into the dog's eyes. "Quigley, we have company. What do we do when we have company? Can you sit for Rylee?"

The dog dropped into a perfect sit, never taking his eyes off his owner. Nick canted his head and arched his eyebrow. "What do we do when we meet a new guest?"

The pup's right paw came up and Rylee squealed with delight. She fell to her knees. "Oh my goodness, he's adorable. Come here, you." The dog jumped into her arms and covered her face with kisses. The dog's excitement thrilled her and she giggled, hugging the live jumping bean as best she could.

"Quigley, let her in the house, will ya?"

The dog's attention immediately returned to his owner.

"Well, he sure makes a bad day better," she said standing and looking around. They stood in a galley kitchen with a square cut out of the wall, like a window, to a small room with a chandelier. Nick had turned the dining room into an office. She followed him into the living room, where comfortable looking furniture and a large screen TV welcomed guests. Quigley jumped up into a corner of the sofa where a blanket was spread.

"Is that his spot?"

Nick turned on lights and snapped on the TV. "Yeah. He's not allowed on any other furniture but there. It's fine though because that's where I usually am."

"Isn't it hard having a dog with your schedule?"

"I think he's used to it now. I pay the girl next door to walk him, feed him when I'm not here for dinner, and pet sit when necessary. She's fourteen and will probably pay cash for a new car on her sixteenth birthday thanks to me. She knows my schedule and on the rare occasions when I work overtime and need her, she's always stepped up. I try not to take advantage, though. That will be the only downside to moving, losing her."

Rylee sat beside Quigley and Nick plopped beside her, scrolling through the guide on the screen to see what was on.

"I'd love to have a dog but my building isn't pet friendly and I'd hate to leave him alone all day."

"You're welcome to visit Quigley any time you like."

She scratched behind his ears. "I might take you up on that. Did you train him?"

"It's a work in progress. He can show you his tricks later. I'd like to be a K-9 officer someday but a lot of things have to fall into place before that happens. For now," he stretched across her lap to pet Quigley's head, "he's my watch dog."

He stopped scrolling on the ballgame. Rylee folded her hands in her lap and they stared at the TV.

"This feels a little awkward." Her voice sounded higher in her ears.

"It doesn't have to be." Nick wrapped his arm around her shoulders and nuzzled her neck. "I'd love to seduce you but if you don't like the idea, we can just watch the game."

His kisses awakened her lower regions and she closed her eyes. They'd laced their conversations with teases and innuendoes about taking their friendship to the next level. Little hints that he'd like to. Her tentative responses that she might, too. Yesterday had changed things. She still wrestled with the notion that it somehow conflicted with her job but, damn it all, she liked having Nick in her circle of friends. Or whatever he was.

"If we did that, I'd be sweaty and sticky for my meeting."

Nick kissed the sweet spot just below her ear. "We can shower."

Her heart pounded. Could he hear it? She laced her fingers with his. "I thought we were just going to be friends?"

Nick slid off the couch and crawled between her knees, placing his hands on her bottom and tugging her toward him. He reached for her face, entwining his fingers in her hair and drew her mouth to his. "It's too late for that."

The kiss was hot. Sensual. Wet when his tongue probed her lips and then slid into her mouth. Her arms wrapped around his neck and feelings she suppressed for so long awakened.

He kissed her longingly, as if he was starved for affection. Short kisses. Long kisses. Deep, stroking kisses. She was equally as hungry and returned his passion. His hands moved up her back, beneath her shirt, heating every inch of skin he caressed. He unhooked her bra and slid one hand around to her breast, lightly rubbing her nipple with the palm of his hand, barely touching it. It electrified her.

"You're so soft." He whispered his words. "Can I take this off?"

"No, Nick."

He immediately dropped his hands and sat back on his haunches, his eyes wide. "No?"

She grinned at the puzzled look on his face and took his hands in hers. "No, we can't do this in front of the dog. What would he think?"

Nick rolled his eyes and regarded the sleeping pup. "Jesus, you drive me crazy. I took him to the dog park this afternoon. He's sound asleep. But if you're worried about it, would you like to relocate to my bedroom?"

Hell yeah, she would. Her insides felt like an improvised explosive device had detonated. She stood on quivering legs to look up at him, certain he could hear her roaring heart.

Wordlessly, he took her hand and led her down the hall to the master bedroom. A king bed, bureau and matching nightstand were the only pieces of furniture in the room. A large screen TV hung on the wall opposite the bed.

Her palms were sweaty. Her ears were ringing. "This room is a good size, nice and manly looking. It—"

Nick drew her into his arms. "I know you're nervous, honey. Shut up, will ya?" His mouth swooped down to cover hers and his kiss simultaneously emptied her lungs of air and filled her soul with the oxygen she'd need to survive going forward. She melted into his embrace. She was safe here. And judging by the erection he pressed against her thigh, she was wanted, too.

He walked her backward until her legs hit the bed, braced her lower back with one hand and lowered her to the bedspread. His lips moved over her cheeks, her chin, beneath her jaw and to the hollow of her neck. Her skin tingled everywhere he touched.

He rolled his hand over her chest. "May I take this off now?" Without waiting for permission, he began unbuttoning her shirt. She ran her hands down his back, grabbed the hem of his sweatshirt, and drew it up toward his shoulders. He rose slightly, reached behind his neck, and dragged it over his head.

Sweet Jesus. She ran her hands along his arms. He was muscular, but not overdeveloped. She caressed bulging biceps and firm shoulders, stroking his taut skin. Her finger outlined the tattoo. His back muscles tightened when he placed both hands on her waist and scooted her up toward the headboard. Opening her shirt and lowering her bra, he covered one breast with his mouth, teasing her nipple with his tongue. His hand moved to the snap on her jeans. Likewise, she worked to unbutton his pants, sliding her hand between fabric and skin to stroke his tight butt.

Nick released her to slip her pants and panties down her legs.

"Nicky, I am nervous. I haven't been with anyone for a while."

"Me either." He dropped her clothes to the floor. "You're beautiful." His hand rolled up her leg to her thigh and then her waist. "Are you on birth control?"

She gulped. "No."

"It's okay, I've got this." He stood and dropped his jeans and shorts to the floor. It was her first look at him naked and the fireworks that soared through her body shocked her. Broad in the shoulders, narrow at the waist, every inch of him toned. His desire obvious. Wetness pooled between her legs.

Nick retrieved a condom from the nightstand and rolled it into place. She scanned his body with her eyes, memorizing every magnificent inch. He moved between her legs and lowered himself gently, hovering above her.

He kissed one side of her mouth and then the other. "I'm a little blessed when it comes to anatomy," he whispered. "I don't want to hurt you so we'll take this slow. Tell me if I need to stop."

She held her breath and felt the tip of his erection probing.

She reached down to guide him into place. Her eyes widened at his girth.

"Relax, honey. I want you real bad. I'll be careful." He eased inside her, bit by bit, each speck of progress catapulting her to a higher plane. She clung to him, wrapping her legs around his waist, and arching her hips to accommodate him. He filled her, gazing into her eyes. "Are you okay?"

Words couldn't express the sensations, the excitement, the desire for more. She nodded and drew his face to hers for another kiss. He settled in deeper and she gasped.

"Tell me if I'm hurting you."

"My God, you're not hurting me. You're sending me to the moon. I've never felt like this."

His hips pushed forward, deeper, tighter. She held her breath. He rocked her slowly, methodically, teasing her inner most regions, spiking her heart rate to volcanic level, speeding up her breathing.

"I want to please you," he whispered, "tell me how you like it."

She could barely think. All she could do was feel him inside her and all around her. "Slow and deep. I think you're there."

He smiled, carefully pressing into her one final inch. Her head dropped back onto the pillow, her eyes closed and she exploded, pulsating around him with such force, she screamed his name. She was vaguely aware the dog had run into the room, more focused on Nick and his unhurried, deliberate gyrations creating spasms that consumed her.

Panting, she opened her eyes to find his face inches from hers, smiling, his eyes a deeper gray. "Oh my God, Nicky."

He kissed her lightly. "Can you do that for me again?"

She blew out her breath. "I might die!"

His smile widened. "I wouldn't let that happen." He slid his hand beneath her and lifted her hips. Every nerve cell in her body sprang to life again. He drove into her with cautious thrusts at first, gaining in intensity and speed as he headed toward satisfaction. They shattered the silence in the room together, she once again screaming his name and he praising a higher power. Quigley howled.

Gradually, they calmed, wrapped in a sheen of sweat, their breaths mingling, their bodies shuddering. Nick gazed into her eyes. "You're in trouble, lady, I've got it bad for you."

Her heart skipped. She felt...something incredible.

He rolled onto his back, removed the condom, and walked to the bathroom to dispose of it. The rear view looked delicious.

Watching him return, she licked her lips. He patted Quigley on the head, and crawled into bed, dragging the sheet over them. She rolled into his outstretched arm and laid her head on his chest. "I'm a spaghetti noodle. I have no bones left."

He chuckled.

"Will it sound corny if I say no one has ever done that to me before? I'm still floating."

He kissed the top of her head. "Not corny. I want to do it again. Give me a minute."

She looked into his eyes. "Do you think this was a good idea?"

"It's the best idea I've ever had."

"Yeah, well, my bosses would disagree. If they found out—"

"I won't let you stop this when it's just started because of some perceived idea you have about conflict of interest. When you're on the job, you don't get your information from the beat cop. I've never given you a story and that's not going to change. Everyone in the building, including the janitor, knows the reporters talk to the chief or the deputy chief. We're both professionals and there's no reason for us to cross that line. If you show up at an accident or other incident that I'm working, I'm not going to treat you differently just because we're together."

"I know, but what will the other guys in the department think? Will they question your loyalty?"

"They'll think I'm one lucky son of a bitch." He rolled on top of her and looked into her eyes. "Give this a chance. We can keep it low-key." His kiss wiped away her concerns. She was ready for round three.

He checked the clock on the nightstand, whispered "damn", and kissed the tip of her nose. "Go get cleaned up before I can't control myself and make love to you again. You don't want to be late." He kissed her sweetly one more time. "You can take a shower if you want."

"Thanks. I'll just wash up."

She stood but didn't leave the side of the bed. "Nicky, I don't sleep around."

His gaze roamed her body and he smiled. "I didn't think you did."

"So," her index finger moved from her to him and back, "this is a 'thing' now?"

He rolled toward her, stood, and swatted her bottom playfully. "You bet your sweet ass it is. Get moving. We can grab a cup of coffee and maybe a little something to eat. Are you hungry? I could eat something."

She strolled to the bathroom knowing he watched her walk naked and feeling sexy as hell. She was too nervous about meeting Dickey's friends to eat anything but she'd never say no to coffee.

A HALF HOUR LATER, they sat at a local coffee shop, Nick wolfing down a raspberry pastry and she nursing a mocha latte.

"Are you coming back to my place after this interview? I'd like it if you did."

"I should go home. I don't even have a toothbrush with me."

"We could stop at a drugstore for one." He shrugged when

she gave him the stink eye. "I already feel the emptiness of my bed. Dinner tomorrow night and you for dessert?"

Her stomach cartwheeled. "How about if I cook dinner for you? And bring my toothbrush."

Just as Nick grinned and opened his mouth to respond, two men passed their table, the second one stopping to take three steps backward. His hand shot out. "Hey, Coop. Long time no see."

Nick stood and reached for his hand. "Benny! It's good to see you, man." They embraced. "How ya been?"

The man nodded, turning his attention toward her. Nick introduced her.

"This is Rylee Lapiz. Rylee, this is my good friend Ben. He's a corrections officer at the jail."

Another cop. She shook his hand and canted her head when he continued to stare.

"From the TV station?"

Oh boy. Here's what she worried about. She nodded.

"Rylee has a midnight interview tonight at *The Last Sip Saloon*," Nick said. "I didn't think she should go alone."

By now, the second man returned and Ben introduced him. Cop number three. "That's a hell of a place to conduct an interview. Nick's right, you shouldn't go there by yourself." He looked at Nick. "You want back up? We were just going to prowl around. We could hang there."

And just like that, she had three police officers watching her six as she walked into the saloon. Ben and his friend were at the bar. They saw them and barely nodded. Nick held her hand through the parking lot and to where Ben and his friend sat, then left her to walk unaccompanied toward the rowdy gathering.

Dickey's crew was whooping it up in the corner as usual. The catcalls and whistles started when they spotted her. The man who'd driven the red car waved her on. Sour Breath.

"Glad you could make it TV Lady. Want a beer?" They gathered around her. She must be getting used to their habit of surrounding her because she didn't flinch.

"No, no thank you."

"Aw, c'mon, one beer ain't gonna hurt youze none. We're givin' ya the scoop of the century. You can at least have a cold one with us."

"No, thanks. I don't drink when I'm working."

The man she remembered as Ape Number One, the one who'd tried to intimidate her by moving into her space, stepped up beside her. Too close to be comfortable. Was Nick watching? If he was still at the bar with Ben, his back was to her.

"You ain't workin' right now, missy. This is, what do you call it, off the record. Let me look in that bag. You ain't got no recorder or anything running, do you?"

He yanked her tote from her shoulder and rummaged through it. She stole a glance in Nick's direction. All three men were on their feet, watching. Ben's hand was on Nick's arm, as if holding him back. Nick wouldn't let them hurt her.

Satisfied there wasn't a recorder in her bag, Number One shoved it back into her arms. "What we tell you tonight, we deny tomorrow. You got that?"

Her heart skipped. This wasn't a ruse. "I understand. But I don't want a drink. Why did you ask me to meet you tonight?"

Two of the group snickered. "How about for a little fun?"

This wasn't what she was here for. "Fuck you, jackass." She turned on Sour Breath. "Either you have something to tell me or you don't. I'm not interested in entertaining you and I won't play your games."

"All right, all right." His hands went up in the air, a beer bottle in the right. "Can't blame us for enjoying the spotlight. You're famous."

"I'm not."

"Well, we think you are. Listen, they done Dickey wrong, ya

know? He was just going along with them, like he didn't know it was for real. It was a fuckin' joke, for shit's sake. We all knew that."

A joke? That's how Dickey's mother described the strange car in the driveway.

"Going along with what?"

"None of us believed him," Ape Number One said. "Dickey was always talking out of his ass. He was a blowhole but he wouldna ratted them out."

Heads all around nodded.

Sour Breath spoke. "It was all fun and games, braggin' about how they trusted him, how he'd handle himself in that situation, ya know? He talked big. But when he found that woman, he was scared shitless."

Number One leaned in. "That din't matter. Dickey would'na said a word. He was no snitch."

Holy hell, what was he saying? "Who? Who are you talking about?"

Sour Breath shrugged. "That's what you have to figure out. Older than Dickey. A little classier, though we got our own kinda class." More head nods. "But he promised to bring us along with him."

"Yeah, he did," one of them mumbled.

"That ain't happenin' now," another one said.

Rylee kept her focus on Sour Breath. "What do you mean? Bring you along where? With whom?"

Number One chuckled, "Yeah, man, with *whom*?" He emphasized the last word to the hooting of the group. She glared at him then nodded for Sour Breath to continue.

"He got hooked up with a big shot. Someone important in City Hall. Called him Daddio. Said—"

She peered at him with one eye closed. "Like that old sitcom twenty years ago? No one says that anymore."

"You got me. That's what he called him. Said he'd done a couple small jobs for him that paid good. Never said what but he—"

"Yeah," Ape Number Two interrupted, "he took us all out to that fancy steakhouse, you know, the one with the two first names. And he picked up the whole fuckin' tab. He was rollin' in Benjamins. We ate like kings that night." He raised his beer bottle. "To fuckin' Dickey!"

They all hollered his name and saluted their dead friend.

She reined in their enthusiasm. "Tell me more about Daddio. Do you know his real name?"

Ape Number One poked her shoulder. "You gotta find that out on your own. We're givin' you pieces. Put them together."

Sour Breath nodded. "He's a high roller in town. Dickey did a little dealin' sometimes and Daddio has a taste for nose candy. He got Dickey on the county payroll. Or it mighta been the city. Like he had a real job."

The group howled with laughter. "That mo-fo never worked a fuckin' day in his life but damn if he didn't get a paycheck."

This didn't make sense. She'd done a public records search on Richard Sharpei once she obtained the police report identifying him. It said he was unemployed, living with his parents. It certainly didn't identify him as a county or city employee. "Are you sure?"

Sour Breath sneered. "'Course I'm sure. Dickey thought he had it made, thought it was all a joke about a body in the trunk, like some kind of allegiance quiz. So, he said yeah, he could get rid a one."

His words stunned her and she took a step backward. He'd told the police he didn't know anything about Jane Doe.

Number Two spoke up. "We got a good laugh about it. Even gave him some options. We—"

"Options? What kind of options?"

He poked her shoulder. "You know that construction site in the North Hills? Make a good place to dump a body. Or drive it out to Ohiopyle State Park and leave it. I volunteered to follow him. Dickey thought small, though, he said Moraine."

Dear God, she was just there yesterday.

Another man chimed in, "I said a car fire at the junkyard. Dickey liked that idea. He had a thing for flames."

She couldn't believe her ears. "These were all plans Dickey had? Any others?"

Number One sneered. "Drive the car into the Allegheny."

A chill crawled up her spine. Like Tessa's car? Was Tessa dead? But she'd met her for dinner after Jane Doe was discovered so it wasn't her in the trunk. Still, Tessa was off the grid.

"Was he really going to go through with it?"

Sour Breath shook his head. "Nah, it was just shit talk, you know. Dickey said Daddio wanted him to do it but we all knew Dickey didn't have the balls to do something like that. He was more on the weasel side. Couldn't figure out how Daddio singled him out as someone who would. And we were right, weren't we boys?" He raised his bottle and the group mimicked him, offering another toast to their dead comrade.

"You don't know how he met Daddio? Or where?"

"Nope. Just that he's connected. And it was his old lady he wanted to snuff."

Rylee's brain worked overtime. "The dead woman was Daddio's wife? And Dickey knew her?"

Sour Breath raised his hands to stop her. "Whoa, we don't know that. Dickey didn't know his old lady, never seen her. From what he said, there was no face for him to recognize even if he did know her. That's when he fucked up, though. He shoulda never called Five-O."

Number Two slammed his empty bottle on the bar. "And that's why he's dead. They fucked him. So you, little lady," he said pointing a dirty fingernail at her face, "gotta do something about it. You were nice to him. You didn't look down your nose at him. It's your job to avenge Dickey."

She was speechless. "What do you expect me to do? You should tell all this to the police."

"We can't, lady." Sour Breath shrugged. "We ain't goin' down as accomplices. I got a record. So does he." His head inclined toward one of the men. "You don't know our names so you can't rat us out. Just do what you do and help Dickey. I seen you on TV, you're good."

He took a long swig of beer and jerked to attention when two men entered the bar. "That's all you get. Keep us out of it. Don't come here talkin' to us again. Go kick ass."

With that, she was dismissed. To a man, they turned their backs to her and began a conversation as if she wasn't right behind them. She turned to see Nick at a high-top table two feet away, far enough that he couldn't have heard the conversation over the bar noise but near enough to reach her in a nanosecond.

He stood as she neared him, took her elbow, and walked her out the door. Once outside, he wrapped his arm around her shoulders. "Benny and his buddy are staying there for a while, just to make sure they don't follow you. Did you get what you needed? Jesus, you're trembling." He drew her closer.

"I don't know."

"Wanna talk about it?"

"I'm not sure. Maybe tomorrow after I straighten it out in my mind."

He walked her to her car. "I wish you'd come back to my place. It's late and I don't like the idea of you driving home alone."

"I've driven in the dark before. Don't start babying me."

He pursed his lips. "Okay, sorry, but call me when you're in your apartment with the door locked. I want to hear your voice before I fall asleep."

"I will. Thanks for tonight. It was phenomenal."

He drew her into his arms. "We'll do it again tomorrow." After a long, heart-stopping kiss, he released her. "Drive safe."

12

She didn't sleep. After an hour of trying, she sat up in bed, crossed her legs to prop open her laptop and created a new document. She wrote in stream of consciousness, the key phrases from Dickey's friends flowing from her fingertips, cringing yet again at the more jarring parts.

Get rid of a body.
Dump it at a construction site.
Drive it into the Allegheny River.

It was four o'clock in the morning but she dialed Tessa's number anyway. Her voice mailbox was full. Dammit Tessa, what happened to you?

This wasn't anything she could report on the news. There was no proof that what Dickey's friends said was true. She couldn't reveal her sources because Sour Breath was right, she didn't know their names. Could Elliott identify them? No matter. What could she tell viewers? That a murdered man from the suburbs claimed to be assigned the task of disposing of a body and a body was found in that same man's driveway. The dots didn't connect.

She should have gone home with Nick and picked his cop's

brain. Well, too late for that. They said Dickey was on a public payroll. Tomorrow, or rather in a few hours, she'd go to City Hall and search the employee records. She'd tell her boss she had a lead on a human-interest story. There was always a charity or benevolent organization there doing something to give viewers the "feel goods."

Her hamster brain continued running.

Who in City Hall could be connected to Dickey? His parole officer? The narcotics cop who initially arrested him? The public defender who handled his case? Parker or Chaney? It wouldn't be the first time a cop erased a confidential informant.

Nah, that was ridiculous. Parker and Chaney were the good guys, like Nick. Had they touched base with the courthouse personnel who'd had dealings with Dickey? Did those folks have wives or girlfriends who were unaccounted for? Old Lady didn't necessarily mean spouse in Dickey's world. It would take some digging, but she could figure out the answers to all of those questions.

What about telling Parker Bentley about tonight's conversation? Did she trust her? If Nick was related to Steel Chaney, maybe he could be an avenue of communication. But that crossed the relationship line they'd established. And their relationship had taken a huge step tonight. She wouldn't jeopardize it.

Maybe call Parker tomorrow and start by asking if there were any updates to the missing person reports. Get a feel for where she and Chaney were on the case. If Jane Doe was the wife of someone with connections, as Sour Breath claimed, certainly someone missed her by now.

EXTRA-LARGE COFFEE CUP IN HAND, Rylee was outside the human resources office promptly at nine. The name of any employee who worked for the city or county was public record. She punched up the files and searched Sharpei. Nothing. Maybe they'd reversed his name. She typed Richard and sorted through more than fifty variations of the name—Richards, Richardson, Richardsen, Rich, Richey. Another goose egg. She stared at the computer screen, clearing the search bar and typed Dickey's last name again. S-h-a-r-p...

The hand on her shoulder stopped her fingers and her heart. "Rylee, my dear, you're at it early today."

Peter Owens, aka The Joker, grinned. He glanced at the screen and then focused on her. "What are you searching for? Can I be of assistance?"

Why would he be familiar with county or city personnel records? He didn't work here, even though he was always walking the halls.

"Good morning Mr. Owens, how are you? She minimized the screen and stood to block it. "I heard a city employee fell on hard times but I didn't learn the full name. I was taking a shot at finding it. You're here awfully early yourself. Is the car business slow this week?"

He eyed her notebook laying open on the desk and nodded. "I have good people running my business. It allows me to focus on my other enterprises. What's the employee's name, maybe I heard it."

She shrugged. "That's all right. My editor wasn't keen on the story idea anyway. Too sappy."

"Ahh, okay. Well, will you be leaving? I'll walk you out of the building."

"No, actually, I, um, I'm waiting for the head clerk to verify the city manager's hiring date. Someone left an anonymous tip that he was working two jobs or something like that." She shrugged her shoulders, trying to play dumb. "I didn't take the message. You know how it is when an enemy is out to make trouble. I'm sure it's incorrect information but it needs verified."

"I see." He stole one more look at the desk, then checked his very expensive looking watch. "Well, I have an appointment so, I'll be going. Would you like to have dinner tonight? I'm flying solo, remember?"

She cringed. "I'm sorry, I have plans."

He stared at her, his eyes narrowing just a bit, then grinned. "Another time." He patted her arm and strode away.

Rylee fell into her chair and exhaled heavily. The man acted creepier every time she saw him. She jostled the mouse to awaken the computer screen. Holy shit, there it was. R. Sharp. Place of residence listed the Sharpei address. Who put Dickey on the public payroll with a false name? What did they use for identification? It listed him as working in the sanitation department. One phone call would verify that.

Rylee cleared the search bar again and, on a hunch, typed Owens. Fewer results than Richards but still at least a dozen. She scanned down to the Ps. No Peter. But the Ts showed on the screen. T. Owens. The address listed was Tessa's. What the actual hell?

Rylee closed the search, maneuvered the mouse to the top of the screen and cleared the search history. Just in case anyone was curious about her visit today.

She strolled to the City Hall receptionist, mulling over her next move. She always chatted with the woman when she was in the building. Amy was like a bartender or hair stylist. She heard the gossip and knew the stories.

"Hey Ams, how are you today? Think you can help a desperate news chaser this morning?" Amy's circular face looked rounder when she smiled.

"I'm looking for a sweet human interest story. Something that will make viewers feel good." Amy's idea was perfect. A family who lost their home in a fire last month and was living in their car. The firefighters had started a fund page for them and Rylee eagerly reported the success of the account so far, the circumstances that had befallen the family and, in a lucky break, located the family and interviewed them. While she loved reporting crime, chances were the fund balance would double or even triple after her report aired. She'd help the family of four back to their feet. That was a good feeling.

Her editor was happy and her day had freed up. Back to a more difficult task. Dickey Sharpei. Maybe he'd kept a pay stub or had an employee identification badge. There had to be some clue about his job. She bet on Janet Sharpei's vanity and called her. After identifying herself and asking how she was doing, Rylee asked about Dickey's belongings.

"What do you mean?" a puzzled Janet Sharpei asked.

"I'm wondering if you went through his personal items when you cleaned out his room."

"Why do you ask?"

How could she answer this without damaging her son's reputation? "The police seem to be nowhere in solving his murder. Did they search his room? Or did you?"

"I haven't been in there." Her tone was short-tempered.

"Did the police search the room?"

She exhaled into the phone. "I think so. It's all a blur. They told us not to disturb anything in there. I'm happy to stay out."

"I understand. Did they take anything? Did they leave you an inventory of the items?"

A lighter clicked and breath filled Rylee's ear. "I think there is a list around here somewhere."

"Would you mind if I stopped over and looked at the list? It will only take a half hour, maybe less. I can come whenever it's convenient for you."

"Is this for another news report? I look a mess. What do you want with it?"

"I'm not sure exactly, Mrs. Sharpei. I want justice for Dickey, I guess."

There was a pause. "You're the only friend who does."

She wasn't exactly Dickey's friend but there was no point in correcting the woman. She headed to the Sharpei home, assuring Mrs. Sharpei she wasn't bringing a camera crew.

It creeped her out shifting her car into park in the same spot the Chevy had occupied. It was hard to fathom that a murdered woman and murdered man had both been in this driveway just a week ago. There was no sign of any of that. The yellow police caution tape was gone. Sophie Ward's house was locked up tight. Life went on as usual on the suburban street.

Mrs. Sharpei greeted her at the door with a clear drink in her hand. A voice in Rylee's head whispered *give her a break, it could be water with ice.* "Did you locate the inventory list?"

"Yes, but I don't see anything on it that is unusual." She flung the multi-page catalog toward her and invited her inside. Rylee scanned it, seeing mostly Dickey's clothes, shoes and the urine-stained pants among the items police deemed important. That would make sense if they thought Dickey had killed Jane Doe. Did they?

The inventory list did not include a wallet, nor any type of official ID.

"Mrs. Sharpei, I ask this with the utmost respect in mind. You said you haven't been into your son's room since..." Janet Sharpei raised bloodshot eyes toward her. "Would you mind terribly if I went in there, just to look around?"

"What are you looking for?"

She shrugged. "I don't know, to be honest. May I see it?"

Mrs. Sharpei waved her hand in the air. "Top of the stairs on the left. Close the door when you're done."

Dickey's room stunk. Rylee stood in the middle of it and turned slowly in a circle, her eyes inspecting the walls, the furniture, the pile of unwashed clothes in the corner that didn't interest the police, and the four-drawer bureau. Surely detectives Chaney and Bentley searched it. She carefully removed the top drawer, looked behind it, underneath it and to the back.

Socks and underwear filled it. She repeated the steps for the lower drawer, looking at the contents first and then inspecting the drawer itself. The top left-hand drawer dragged when she drew it out, hung up, and she had to close it and reopen it again, yanking and lifting it upward to slide it out. This one held T-shirts with tattered necks and stains.

She ran her hand along the bottom, caught a corner of something and raised the drawer higher to look under it. Her tugging had ripped the brown under backing on the drawer, revealing it as a false bottom. Cautiously, she peeled it back an inch and then another.

Holy shit. Taped to the real bottom of the drawer was a baggie with maybe fifty pills inside and a plastic card. It was a driver's license for R. Sharp with Dickey's picture. She snapped a photo on her phone of both.

Just to be thorough, she reexamined the other drawers but none of them had false layers. She rummaged through Dickey's closet touching everything, testing to see if there were more hiding spots. It smelled like a gym locker and she yanked her shirt up over her nose. She should be wearing gloves. Some of his stuff was filthy. And now her fingerprints were all over it.

Mrs. Sharpei was nursing a drink with a lime when she came down the stairs. Doubtful it was water. "Did you find what you were looking for?"

Truth be told, she wasn't sure what she'd stumbled on and she didn't intend to add to this woman's misery. She avoided answering. "May I ask you a personal question? How do you know Peter Owens?"

Her face crinkled. "The car man?"

"Yes."

"I don't know him. Why?"

"He came to the funeral home and paid his respects. I saw you talking to him."

Her hand swayed in the air. "My doctor prescribed an antidepressant for me. That whole ordeal is a blur. I barely remember it."

The alcohol probably didn't help either.

"One more thing. You said Dickey didn't drive, right?"

"Not anymore. His license was suspended. His friends always picked him up. That's why it was so absurd for them to think he'd drive that car away."

"Yes ma'am it was. Thank you for your time."

13

Parker reached for the mocha latte Chaney carried. "You're a good man. How'd it go in court yesterday?"

He nodded. "As predicted. ADA Moore added another notch to her belt. That drunk driver will never kill anyone again. I have a love-hate relationship with that woman. Yesterday, she couldn't do anything wrong. What'd I miss here?"

"Not much. I tried to regroup. Except for the performance by Dickey's buddies, his funeral was a non-moment. I didn't even get a glimpse of one license plate to figure out who they are. I should have gotten out there faster to talk to them."

Chaney gestured away her doubt.

"I took pictures of the Visitor's Book and reviewed every name who signed in, but no one stands out. Obviously, none of his buds signed it. I can't tell you how many social media accounts I was on. They were all dead ends. There has to be a clue somewhere, Steel. No one gets away with two murders."

He grinned. "You're right. And we may have found it. We have an anorexic lead."

"Anorexic?"

"Yeah, it's thin but it's something. The coroner recovered a small piece of a back molar, specifically the right permanent mandibular second molar, also known as number thirty-one. It was smashed into her gums."

"Christ, partner, way to bury the lead. When did you find out? That should have been the first thing out of your mouth, you numbnut."

"Okay, okay. I only got the call while I was getting coffee. Here's what I think we do. Jane Doe didn't look like a criminal so it's a long shot but we can submit a request to the FBI's National Dental Image Repository. If she's in NCIC, we'll get a hit."

Bentley stared at him. "You think Jane Doe is in the National Crime Information Center? What about the woman leads you to that conclusion?"

"Nothing. But you never know. People can surprise you. What else have we got?"

Bentley grunted. They had nothing. Just a hooded form that seemed to disappear in the darkness. The requested traffic camera footage was being reviewed but the interdepartmental red tape was strangling.

Missing persons was still a negative. "How can no one miss this woman? She wasn't homeless or a vagrant, not the way she was dressed. Homeless women don't get manicures and pedicures or wear expensive jewelry. Maybe she didn't work for an employer to miss her but surely she had friends. I don't get it."

Chaney stared at her. "Don't you have friends that you don't see or talk to for weeks, maybe longer? It's only been a few days."

"It's been more than a week. What if we make a public appeal? I could call Rylee Lapiz."

Chaney didn't like that idea. "We don't want the media doing our job. What if we wait and see what today brings? Maybe one of your tips will pan out."

As if on cue, Parker's cell rang. "Christ, she must be psychic. It's Rylee Lapiz." She slid her finger across the screen to accept the call and tapped the speaker button.

"Hey, Rylee, what do you know? You're on speaker."

"Can you take me off speaker, please?"

She stared at Chaney, shrugged, and tapped the speaker button. Then she moved next to Chaney and held the phone at face level. "Okay, what's up?"

"Any chance I can buy you a cup of coffee sometime today? One hundred percent off the record? It's important."

Chaney's eyebrows shot up.

"How come?" She'd never met with Rylee one-on-one nor any member of the media, for that matter. This request was out of the blue and unusual. Except for the night they were both drunk, Rylee kept her personal life personal, just like she did.

"I want to talk to you. Not on the phone. I swear this is on the level, I'm not trying to trick you into giving me a story or anything. I've learned something that I think you should know. Maybe you already do and you can help me sort it out. Totally off the record. You can pick the meet."

"Learned something pertaining to what?"

"I don't want to say."

"You in some kind of trouble?"

"No. More like I'm troubled by something."

She eyed Chaney. "Okay if I bring Detective Chaney?"

"I'd rather you didn't. I trust you."

Chaney acted insulted and she grinned.

"This sounds serious."

"Serious as a heart attack."

"All right, I think I can manage to get away. How about around three? *Your Coffee Cup* sound good?" The place had an extensive coffee menu.

"Thanks. I'll be there."

Chaney waited to make sure the call ended. "What's that all about?"

"Your guess is as good as mine. She sounded off, though, don't you think?"

He agreed. "Maybe she wants love life advice about dating a cop. I think she's seeing my cousin, Nick. He's a beat cop downtown."

"Can't imagine she'd ask to meet me on company time. That would be more like a drink after work convo."

"Want me to give him a call?"

"Nah, it's probably not important. I'll find out in a couple hours. Let's take another look at the folks who paid their respects to Dickey."

Admittedly, Bentley was a little uncomfortable meeting a news reporter, even for an off-the-record conversation. Sure, Rylee Lapiz seemed different from the other bloodhounds who chased the ambulances and used voice intonations to imply what the facts didn't always support. Rylee dug for the truth and reported it as such without embellishment. Beyond the night the two of them stumbled out of the nightclub together, she hardly knew the woman. She sipped her latte and watched over the rim as Rylee approached, her own cup steaming in her hand.

"Hi, thanks for meeting me."

"Sure thing. What's up?"

Rylee laid her phone on the table and held open her tote. "I'm turning off my phone." She picked it up and held the buttons on both sides, then demonstrated as she swiped it off. "You can check my bag to make sure I'm not recording this."

Parker felt her eyebrows come together. "What's this about?"

Rylee looked around, closed her hands around her cup and leaned in. "I really wrestled with talking to you. I'm all about my job but I also think facts are important to both our jobs." Her chest expanded with the breath she inhaled. "Are you anywhere close to identifying Jane Doe?"

Parker expelled her own audible breath. "For fuck's sake, Lapiz, is this a damn fishing expedition? I've got better things to do with my time."

"It's not, I swear it's not. I think I know something." She lifted her cascading hair with both hands, coaxing it behind her ears. "I don't know what it is I know and I can't tell you how I know it but—"

"Then this meeting is over."

Rylee reached across the table and grabbed her wrist. "Please, give me this. Do you have anything on her?"

She'd never seen Rylee look scared. Or heard her beg for information. Her police training told her to repeat the standard line, the case was under investigation and no information was being released at this time. Her instinct said otherwise. "No."

Rylee's shoulders sagged. "Have you been able to determine if she was married?"

"How would we do that if we don't know who she is? Have you been able to figure that out?"

Rylee's complexion paled. "Remember, I can't be your source for this. I'm merely sharing a concern with you. I'll deny we ever spoke."

"Okay, okay. If I can protect you, I will. Was Jane Doe married?"

"Yes, I think she was. And I think Dickey Sharpei was part of a plan to kill her and get rid of her body. He was just a puppet though and someone big, someone important is, or was, working his strings."

Parker's stomach dropped. "How do you know this?"

"I can't tell you that, but—"

"What do you mean you can't tell me? What are we here for?"

Her cheeks reddened. "Not for me to do your damn job. Will you listen to me, please?"

Parker bit back her retort. *Catch more flies with honey*, she reminded herself. She folded her hands in front of her on the table. "Okay, I'm listening."

"Dickey knew a mysterious car was going to manifest itself in his driveway with a woman's body inside. He—"

"How the hell do you know that?"

Rylee stared at her. "I'm not going to reveal my sources."

"This is a murder investigation. You damn well better tell me what you're basing this on."

"I won't."

"I can subpoena your notes."

"There are no notes. Will you shut up and hear me out?"

They stared at each other, both refusing to blink, each breathing a little harder. Finally, Parker nodded.

"Dickey lied to you. Finding Jane Doe was a surprise but it wasn't out of the blue. She wasn't just anybody, she was *someone*. And he screwed up when he didn't do his part and that's why he's dead. Figure out who she is and you find out who killed Dickey or had him killed. Because I don't think this person is the hands-on type. He designates." She pinched her fingertips into her temples, as if her head ached.

"You don't have anything on Jane Doe? Not clothing tags or medical scars or anything? Breast implants that you can trace back? Nothing?"

Parker laughed in a way that bordered on sarcasm. "How would you know about all that?"

Rylee's frown disappeared. "I take my job seriously. I took a couple of criminology courses and I read a lot."

Now the veracity of her news reports made sense. "No artificial breasts. Only a partial molar."

Rylee's eyes grew round. "Can you trace it?"

"Not yet. And not if she doesn't have a criminal record."

Rylee looked puzzled, so Parker elaborated. "It's a long shot that she's in the FBI dental registry but we're checking."

"Can't you release a photo to all the dentists and ask them to search their files?"

Well, she was smart but not cop caliber yet. "A monumental endeavor and possible violation of individual privacy rights without cause. But I'm not writing it off as a dead end."

"What if I gave you a suggestion?"

"What d'you mean?"

She shrugged. "If I had a hunch, or a feeling about someone and there was another someone who I couldn't locate and comments had been made that led me to think that maybe my friend was in trouble, like maybe she had something to do with it, could I give you some information and you follow up on it in regards to the Jane Doe investigation?"

"You're talking in riddles."

"Could you?"

"Probably. It depends on what you tell me."

"Maybe I know a connection to Jane Doe that sounds so bizarre when I think it in my head let alone if I'm going to say it out loud but it's this nagging feeling..." Rylee clutched her stomach as if she experienced actual pain.

"You're not making sense. Do you think you know who Jane Doe is?"

Rylee nodded slowly and Parker's coffee percolated in her stomach. She mentally reviewed the law. This was no different than an anonymous tip coming in over the phone. It could be a lead. Getting it to hold up in court would be Laquisha Moore's problem.

"Who?'

Rylee gulped. "I think my friend Tessa Owens has something to do with Jane Doe."

Parker could swear tears threatened to spill. "Owens as in the hotshot car dealer?"

"His daughter."

"Why do you think that? Connected how?"

"I haven't been able to contact her and her car was towed from the Allegheny last week. I know that an option for Dickey to dispose of a body was to ditch the car in the river."

"How do you know that?"

"I can't tell you."

"Jesus, Rylee, if you want me to go off on some crazy tangent you have to justify it."

Rylee canted her head. "No, I don't. I could have called in to your damn hotline and simply left a name. You wouldn't ask so many questions then, you'd just look into it. That's all I'm asking. I'm genuinely concerned about my friend but maybe I should have talked to Detective Chaney or my friend Nick." She reached for her phone and switched it on.

"Okay, wait a minute. Let me get this straight. You can't reach your friend and her husband hasn't reported her missing. Why not? Are you sure—"

Rylee gathered her bag and her cup and stood. "Tessa's not married."

It was her turn to tilt her head. "But you said you thought Jane Doe was married."

Rylee glared at her. "I do. It's her mother. She's missing too."

14

Parker watched Rylee walk away, shocked by her words. Two missing women? One young, Rylee's age. One not so much. Jane Doe was an older woman. The coroner estimated between fifty and sixty. The profile fit.

This was a tip reported by a reliable source. But how to follow up? The easiest would be to contact Peter Owens and ask about the whereabouts of his wife and daughter. But Owens was a politician, even though he didn't currently hold an office. He was ambitious and ruthless and she could envision him rising to a state level office or higher. Not someone's toes you stepped on lightly.

She searched both names on the Internet, finding more social media presence for the daughter than the mother. The daughter's social pages depicted a typical, entitled young woman oversharing personal information like her birthday celebration, favorite band, newest manicure, and a new car from daddy. Was that the car dumped in the river? Parker jotted down the details on her iPad to check when she was back at the office.

There were lots of party pictures, some that included Rylee. Rylee wasn't the one tossing back Fireball shots though or lifting her top for the camera. And a rash of posts berating her mother for various infractions, from ignoring her texts to listing herself on a popular 'single again' dating app, to accusations that she flirted with her boyfriends. Sounded like an interesting family.

Pearl Owens didn't have any media pages under her own name. That didn't mean she wasn't on any sites, especially since the daughter referenced a dating site. Her name appeared in a handful of news articles describing her as estranged from her candidate husband and pursuing a divorce. If successful, Pearl Owens would be well off financially for the rest of her life. She was seeking fifty percent of everything Peter Owens owned. Parker jotted more notes. Easy enough to verify with civil court records.

Based on the stories, Mrs. Owens had run a smear campaign against her husband after discovering he was unfaithful. Peter Owens lost his bid for election to city council. Hmm. That could be a motive to hurt someone.

She called Chaney on her way back to the office. "What do you know about Peter Owens?"

Chaney snorted. "An ambitious s.o.b. I'm not a fan. Why?"

"Rylee says his wife and daughter are in the wind. Missing. She thinks there is a connection between them and Jane Doe."

"What does that mean?"

"That Jane Doe might be the missus."

"Based on what?"

Parker relied on her instinct again. "I've never seen her so off balance. She's all over the place in terms of what she thinks and what she knows, which she isn't completely divulging. She hid behind the usual 'protecting my sources.'" Steel mumbled something unintelligible.

"She can't locate either one of them, which is unusual. She's no dummy and she's been snooping around. She knows enough to reach out for my help. She says Dickey lied to us and that Jane Doe's arrival in his driveway was not unexpected. And she's worried about Tessa and Pearl Owens. That's daughter and mother, respectively. Know them?"

"Just the mother's name from the shit show during the last election. She was all over the news defaming him. I believed every word but what do I know? You don't remember that?"

"I don't pay attention to politics. But I do pay attention to Rylee and this feels reliable."

"Christ, it will be a Pandora's Box if we open it."

"Don't I know it. Still, our priority is to identify Jane Doe. Just for the hell of it, run a license check on Pearl Owens, common spelling. Let's see how old she is. And let's compile a list of dentists in the Owens' neighborhood. They lived on Fox Chapel Road. I'm almost at the office. We can start calling the area dentists to inquire if either of the women were patients. HIPAA is designed to protect a patient's privacy, not his or her identity. If we're lucky enough to find their dentist, we can request a court order based on information received to compare the molar fragment to their records. I'm in the parking garage. I'll be right up."

On call number fifteen, Chaney hit the jackpot. He located the Owens' family dentist who said all three family members were patients on an excellent family plan. It was already close to five o'clock. He convinced the dentist to stay at his office with the promise they'd use their flashing red lights to be there as soon as possible.

They rushed to Chaney's car. "Time to clue in the dragoness, Parker. We can't take this picture of the tooth to him without her knowing. We need a subpoena for his records if he confirms an identity. I'd rather have it in hand than wait for it.

And you know Laquisha, she'll have our hides if all the t's aren't crossed and the i's dotted."

"It's after four. She might already be gone. I might have to call her at home. She's going to ask questions."

"Don't give her the Owens name unless you have to. Tell her we have a lead and we're seeking confirmation. She's clever enough to draft the court order without identifying the person of interest. We don't want the media to get wind of this."

Bentley took a deep breath and dialed the district attorney's office, waited for the call to transfer to Laquisha Moore's personal phone and explained the situation. Thankfully, she caught Laquisha preparing to attend a banquet and received the authorization to proceed with few questions asked. By the time they reached the dentist's office, the subpoena was in her inbox and accessible on her phone.

The dentist was nervous as hell. They saw him pacing as they approached the glass doors to his building. He had all three Owens family members' files spread on his desk.

"Do-do y-you have a warrant?"

Bentley handed him her phone. "In this case, it's a subpoena." He read it excruciatingly slowly.

"All right. Show me what you have, what you think I can identify." He hunched over the files with a magnifying glass, moving from one file to the next to the last and back. Parker scraped her finger against her thumb. Could he take any longer?

He exhaled loudly and straightened. "Yes. I can confirm this fragment is from my patient."

Parker's heart skipped. Finally.

Chaney cleared his throat and gripped the dentist's shoulder. "Sir, we'd like to request that you don't discuss this evening with anyone. This tooth fragment identifies the victim of a homicide. Notifications must be made and our murder investigation has to proceed unencumbered." The way the man paled at his words, he doubted he'd speak about it ever.

He eyed Parker. "What next, Detective?"

She slammed the car door and yanked her seatbelt into place. "Logically, we notify the family. But I want to talk to Rylee Lapiz first. I want to know how she knew Jane Doe was Pearl Owens."

15

Rylee breathed a sigh of relief when Nick walked through *Smitty's* door. All she wanted was this day to be over and to spend time in his arms.

"Sorry, I'm late." He dropped a soft kiss on her mouth. "The lieutenant decided to call an impromptu squad meeting. You look like you need that beer."

He signaled for the waitress to bring two more and slid into the booth beside her.

"I'm not sure all the beer in the world is going to help me tonight. I did something this afternoon that I'm still not sure was the right thing to do. I may have compromised myself."

Nick squeezed her hand. "Talk to me."

His touch reassured her. "I gave Detective Parker Bentley information today that I think pertains to the Jane Doe case. Do you know her?"

"I know who she is, I've never worked with her. I think she's partnered with Steel."

"She is. Let me back up and tell you what Dickey's friends told me."

Nick listened silently as she recounted the conversation, his mouth dropping open at times, his eyebrows hiking.

"I know it sounds bizarre, like a bad mob movie but the more I thought about it, the more I believed it. Why would Dickey's friends make up something like that? They aren't that creative." She filled her lungs and exhaled.

"None of what they claim is information I can report but I felt like I had to do something with it so I met Parker for a coffee and I gave her some crumbs. I didn't reveal my sources. You're the only one who knows who told me all this. I'm trusting you to keep that to yourself."

"You don't have to worry about that, hon. When you say crumbs, what do you mean? How much did you tell her?"

Rylee wrung her hands. "I told her my concerns about Tessa and her mother, that I can't reach Tessa, can't find her anywhere and there's no sign of Pearl. I called Aunt Betty. Tessa isn't there. Aunt Betty hasn't talked to either Tessa or her mom in months. She—"

"Whoa, wait a minute. Beyond being unable to reach Tessa, what makes you think she's gone missing? And when did her mother enter the picture?"

"When I found Peter Owens at home in his bathrobe."

"That's hardly evidence. He was in his own home. He had a right to be there."

She twisted to look him square in the eye. "Something isn't right in that house. I was there. I felt it."

"That's not enough to incriminate the guy."

She laid her hand over their clutched hands. "Someone once told me, when you know, you know."

The corners of his mouth edged up. "Okay, you have me there. You told Parker you're concerned about Tessa and her mother. That has nothing to do with what Dickey's entourage claims. You're good so far. What else did you tell her?"

"That Dickey was part of a plan to dump a body. She was a little miffed that I wouldn't tell her how I knew that. And I told her about Tessa's car being towed from the river, which was a news story so that's not revealing any secrets."

"What else?"

"That's all. I gave her two names, just as if I'd called the anonymous tip line and left them. Except you and I both know those lines are not anonymous. She told me they recovered a partial tooth, not for publication. Hopefully, she searched for Tessa's dentist today."

"And what?"

"And can tell me I'm crazy. That Jane Doe isn't Tessa or her mother. And I sent her on a wild goose chase."

"Okay, what about all that has you questioning your ethics? You don't have the resources to check any of that on your own, do you?"

She shook her head.

"The way I see it, you received information that you tried to verify, just like you do any news story. Did you ask Parker for an exclusive if Jane Doe is identified?"

She shook her head again.

"Then how are you compromised? You may be sitting on a story that you can't confirm and you went to a source to try to get confirmation. Isn't that how you do all your reporting?"

Her shoulders relaxed. Looking at it like that seemed right. She leaned in and kissed his cheek. "Thank you for that. There's something else I know that I didn't share with Parker."

He waited.

"Dickey was on the county payroll under the name R. Sharp. And he had a driver's license in that name."

"Jesus, are you certain?"

"Yep. I found the license in his room today and I saw—"

"Wait. What? You searched his room? When?"

She moved her hair behind her ears. "Sour Breath said Dickey was collecting a check from the city or county, he didn't know which. I was at City Hall when it opened this morning and I searched the records. I found R. Sharp. And T. Owens. Tessa was collecting a paycheck too. I can't believe she didn't tell me because she was terrible at keeping secrets. But she was listed as an employee in the sanitation department, same as Dickey. I verified that with the department supervisor who didn't sound too happy that I was asking.

"And then, out of the blue, Peter Owens showed up, looking over my shoulder and creeping me out. He tried to see what I was doing and asked if he could help. I closed the screen right away but that's when alarms started going off in my head. Who would put Tessa on the payroll? Who paid respects to Dickey? Who seemed unusually close to Janet Sharpei when she said she didn't know him? And where is Pearl Owens?"

"How do you know Mrs. Sharpei doesn't know Owens?"

"I visited her this afternoon. I called her when I left City Hall and asked about Dickey's personal belongings. She allowed me to go to the house and I searched his room and found the license and some drugs. And she said she didn't know Peter Owens. I watched her face. She might have been a little tipsy but I don't think she was lying."

She reached for her phone, tapped on the photo icon, and showed him the driver's license picture and the baggie of pills.

"Holy fuck, girl. Are you telling me you found that license after the police searched his bedroom?"

"Apparently."

"How?"

"There was a false bottom in his bureau. It ripped when I yanked on the drawer."

"I hope you left it where you found it."

"I did."

"Honey, this is a definite lead for investigators, not just bullshit that a bunch of potheads are spewing."

"Don't turn into a cop on me now, Nick."

"I am a cop. And you could be in danger. If you're right and someone killed Dickey because he failed to follow through on a murder scheme, they'll be looking for loose ends. They could be watching Dickey's pals and know you've been talking to them. They could be watching you."

A shiver crawled up her spine. The same sensation she experienced when Peter Owens laid his hand on her shoulder this morning.

"Well, then they know I spoke to Parker. And they know you and I spend time together. They know I have a police presence on my side."

"That's not the point. I want you to be less cavalier about all of this. You could be poking a dangerous bear."

"I think the bear is Peter Owens. I can't explain why and I can't prove it. But he seems to be at the center of all of this. Oh, and I forgot to tell you, he wanted me to go to dinner with him tonight. Who asks their daughter's best friend out on a date? That's just disturbing."

Nick's eyes widened and his head tipped. "He hit on you? Well, now I might have to hurt the low life." When he punctuated his words with a laugh, she laughed too, sensing the tension of the last few minutes fade. He drew her close for a sweet kiss. "I should warn you I'm a jealous man."

She smiled. "I'm okay with that. If you think I'm in danger, maybe you should be my personal bodyguard, just to keep me safe."

"That's my plan. We should go to your apartment and pack some things. You can stay with me for a while, just to be safe."

Her stomach jumped. "Nicky, we don't know each other well enough for that."

"Well, honey, we'll get to know each other real fast. That

apartment door of yours is flimsy and, while the chain lock is a good effort, one swift kick and it will break off the frame. I'd rather you hang out with me and Quigley for a few days or as long as necessary. I'm on daylight through the end of the month so our schedules will coincide. Your gut is already telling you something is wrong so listen to it."

A million thoughts jumbled her brain. Yeah, she enjoyed the hell out of being with this man but living with him was a different matter. Before she could counter his logic, her phone vibrated on the table. Parker Bentley.

She punched accept and hit the speaker button. "Hey, Parker."

"We have to talk."

She had to hear the bar noise in the background. "Okay, sometime tomorrow?"

"Where are you now?" The tone of her voice was ominous.

"Now? It's almost ten o'clock."

"I know what time it is. Where are you?"

"I'm out with a friend."

"Where? With whom?"

"What's going on?"

"I want to talk to you now. Where are you? I'll come to you."

She muted the phone and looked at Nick. "What should I do?"

"She doesn't sound like she's going to take no for an answer. Tell her we'll wait on her."

"I'm at *Smitty's*. It's a local bar near my apartment on Canteen Street."

"I'm on my way."

She disconnected the call and finished her beer. Turning to Nick, her eyes filled with tears. "What if it's bad news about Tessa?"

Nick wrapped his arms around her. "I'm here."

She rested her head on his chest and felt it vibrate when he spoke. "If it is bad news, you're coming home with me. No arguments."

"Okay."

"Do you want another beer?"

"No, I better not. She sounded serious."

The mood in the bar changed the minute they walked in. Parker's stature screamed cop and the look on her face sent a message—don't fuck with me. Behind her, Steel Chaney was an imposing figure, his focus taking in every face and aspect of the bar in seconds and sizing them up.

Rylee sat straighter and placed her hand on Nick's thigh. He clutched it under the table.

Spotting her, Parker stormed to the table, eyed Nick, and stuck out her hand. "Parker Bentley."

Nick shook her hand, recited his name, then grinned at Chaney and nodded. "Cuz." They shook hands and Steel returned the nod. "Cuz."

Rylee smiled, hoping to lighten the mood. "What'd you do, use lights and sirens? That probably cleared the parking lot."

Bentley glared and plopped into the booth sliding over to sit opposite Rylee. Chaney squeezed in beside her. "I want to know what you know about Dickey Sharpei and who told you." She tapped the table with her forefinger. "Now."

Well, hell, this was a showdown at the OK Corral. Rylee grinned, despite the roller coaster rate of her heart. "That's what this is about?" She looked at her watch, then dropped her hand to Nick's thigh again. "At this hour? Why don't you tell me what you know?"

Bentley's nostrils flared, like a bull ready to attack. Chaney leaned in. "We identified Jane Doe."

Rylee caught her breath. "Who is she?"

Chaney stared at her for the longest ten seconds of her life. "It's Pearl Owens."

Every organ inside her chest crashed, dropped like lead

to the bottom of her stomach. Nick's hand moved over hers and gripped it, sending strength up her arm. But it wasn't enough.

Rylee burst into tears. "Oh my God, no. What about Tessa? Where's Tessa?"

Nick's arm wrapped around her shoulder.

"Tessa isn't our concern," Bentley barked. "How did you know?"

"I didn't."

Bentley raised her voice. "Tell me who you talked to."

Rylee straightened her shoulders. "What?" She swiped at her wet cheeks.

"Who was your source of information?"

"I can't tell you that."

"You can and you will."

"Go to hell, Parker. Don't take it out on me because I'm better at my job than you." Nick's hands tightened.

"You could find your ass in jail."

At that, she threw her head back and laughed. "Go ahead. You'll do wonders for my career. I'll probably get an offer for a network job."

Bentley turned her scowl to Nick. "Do you know?"

The slightest smile lifted the corners of his mouth but he remained silent and returned her stare.

Chaney's meaty fist wrapped over Bentley's arm on the table. "Let's slow down here. Everybody take a breath. Rylee, we understand your commitment to protecting your sources and we admire you for that." Bentley's head twisted so quickly, it was a wonder her neck didn't snap.

"But you provided key information in a murder investigation and we're asking for a little more detail. What else can you tell us?"

Bentley's chest heaved, but she didn't speak.

"I've told you everything I'm willing to tell you, Detective.

Besides, my information pertained to Dickey Sharpei, not Pearl Owens. I can't help you."

She stuttered over her best friend's mother's name. Pearl Owens wasn't the classical *Leave It To Beaver* mother but there were memories of ice cream excursions, sleepovers that ended with animal pancakes, and dress-up-make-up days when she and Tessa were allowed to raid Pearl's closet and dabble in her cosmetics case. Now the person who Rylee once thought was the most beautiful woman on earth was dead. Brutally murdered.

Parker spoke up. "We can subpoena your notes."

Distress turned to anger. "Do whatever you want, Parker. Waste your time on me instead of trying to find the person responsible for two murders. Then tell me how you sleep at night. Nick, I'm ready to leave."

He stood and signaled for their waitress. Rylee grabbed her bag and slid to the edge of the seat.

"We're not done talking," Bentley snapped.

Rylee stared at her. "Yes, we are." She took Nick's hand and walked toward the door, praying that her trembling legs wouldn't give out on her. Outside, she fell against his side, grateful for the tight grip he had on her.

"I'll follow you to your apartment." Nick's voice was strong and calm. "Pack an overnight bag. Let's get you home."

"Just for tonight, okay? I'll probably feel better if I'm not alone. As soon as my hands stop shaking, I have to call my boss. I know the identity of Jane Doe and I can report that. Plus, they should know about Parker's threat."

They'd reached her car and Nick looked at her with wide eyes. "You're going to use what they told you tonight?"

The question surprised her. "Did either one of them say the conversation was off the record? Did they ask me not to use the information? Did they not know they were talking to a reporter and identify a murder victim? Why shouldn't I report it?"

Nick shrugged. "No, they didn't say anything like that. I just thought…"

"What? That I'm not going to do my job? You're sleeping with the enemy, remember?"

"No, honey, I didn't think any of that. I apologize. Make your call and let's go. I can't wait to get the enemy home and in bed."

16

Bentley shriveled under Chaney's stare.

"I thought I was mentoring you on police procedure, not people skills. What was all that?"

Bentley scratched at her cuticle. "I blew it. I lost my temper."

"I'll say. Because if that was interrogation of a reluctant witness, we have some work to do."

"I know, I'm sorry."

"It's not me you owe an apology to, it's Rylee."

"She knows more that she could tell us."

"Maybe. But that's not how we work a case. What next, Detective?"

Bentley blew out a breath. "We talk to Peter Owens."

Chaney eased out of the booth. "We notify him of his wife's death. We don't attack him and we don't interrogate him."

Her head bobbed. "Yes, sir. I know, I'm sorry. It won't happen again."

∽

Even though it was after midnight, lights were on at the Owens home and a car was parked in the driveway. Parker rang the bell, knocked, and rang a second time when there was no immediate response.

Finally, a shadow appeared through the beveled glass. The door swung open to reveal Peter Owens in gym shorts dripping water from head to toe. "What the hell?" His demeanor changed the minute he saw them. "Oh, sorry, detectives. I'm entertaining out in the hot tub. I didn't hear the bell. It's late. What are you doing here?"

Parker had never met Peter Owens. She knew him only by reputation. How did he know who they were? She removed her credentials from her back pocket and showed them to him.

"Mr. Owens, I'm Detective Parker Bentley. This is Detective Steel Chaney. May we come in?"

They'd have to avoid the growing puddle around his bare feet. She stared at him, wondering what was odd about the man. Fit for his age. Overly whitened teeth. Hairless. Geez, he shaved his chest. To remove the gray hairs? She locked her lips to keep from smiling.

"What's this about?"

"May we come in?" she repeated.

"Yes, yes, of course. Pardon my manners." He stepped backward and waved them in. "Come in, come in."

From the balcony, a woman called. "Petey? I'm getting lonely out here."

At least Owens had the decency to blush. But he ignored her.

"How can I help you, Detective?"

Parker cleared her throat. "I'm afraid we have some bad news, sir. I'm sorry to tell you we've identified a homicide victim as your wife. I'm very sorry for your loss."

Splashing water noises caught all of their attention and then a rather buxom naked woman appeared in the balcony doorway. "Petey?" Seeing them, she squealed and scampered out of sight.

Owens looked from the sliding glass door to them, grinning like a jock who just scored. "My ex-wife and I are separated and in the midst of a divorce. As you can see, my ex-wife isn't a concern of mine."

Parker felt her jaw drop but she recovered quickly. "Yes, sir. I wonder if we could ask you when the last time was you saw your wife."

"I couldn't tell you."

"What about your daughter? May we speak to her? Is she home?" She hoped not. Not if her father was naked in the hot tub with a woman at least fifteen years younger than him.

"Who? Tessa? Ah, no, she's in Florida visiting her aunt."

Wasn't that convenient? "We'll need to contact her, sir. Can you give me a phone number to reach her?"

He offered a lame laugh. "I don't have the number memorized. No need with a smart phone. But Tessa hasn't been here for some time. She wouldn't know anything about this."

"About what?" Chaney asked.

Owens faltered, but only slightly. "You said her mother was a homicide victim. I'm not a police officer but I watch enough TV to know homicide means murder. Is there anything else?"

Chaney threw the lead back to her with a quick glance. "We'd like to ask you a couple of questions, sir."

"Now? Tonight? You can see I'm otherwise engaged. Is it important?"

His wife of who knew how many years and the mother of his child was murdered and he was asking them if it was important? Parker had a hard time processing that.

"It is, Mr. Owens. Just a few questions."

He rocked from side to side. "Would you mind if I grabbed a robe? I'm catching a chill standing here like this." He pivoted and headed toward a rear room, pointing toward a well-stocked bar. "Help yourself to a drink. At this hour, you can't still be on the clock."

When he was out of sight, she looked at Steel and whispered. "This guy's a piece of work."

"I told you I'm not a fan."

Owens emerged from the room wearing a white cotton bathrobe and matching slippers. He detoured to the balcony, spoke to his guest low enough so they couldn't hear, and closed the door when he re-entered. He approached them with a wide grin. He sailed behind the bar and lifted a crystal glass decanter Parker would bet carried a five-hundred-dollar price tag. He dug a scoop of ice from a stainless-steel ice bucket with its complementing tongs and filled a matching crystal cocktail glass halfway. He held the bottle up to them. "Join me?"

The perfect happy hour host. "No thank you, sir. Despite the hour, we *are* still on duty."

Owens gulped half the drink, set the glass down, then leaned with both elbows on the bar. "I don't know how I can help you."

"Did your wife have any enemies?"

He shrugged. "I don't know the first thing about her anymore."

"You said you're separated. I'm sorry. How long has that been your situation?"

"Don't be sorry, Detective Bentley. Whatever happened to the bitch, she deserved it." Another sip of liquor.

"How long, sir?"

He shrugged again. "Not long enough. Let's see," he scratched the underside of his chin and stared at the ceiling, "it was before the election so I'd guess, maybe, late summer? I don't really know, hon."

Well, that raised her hackles. Beside her, Chaney's shoulders stiffened.

"It's Detective Bentley, sir."

"Yes, yes, of course. Sorry, whenever I'm around a beautiful woman I can't help my endearments. Whatever lured you into this line of work? With your looks, you could be a model."

Jesus, the man was pompous. "Do you recall when the last time was you saw her or spoke to her?"

"No, I don't."

"Do you know where she was living?"

The glass jiggled in his hand, the ice clinked against the side, and he quickly set it down. "Up until recently, she was living here."

"When did she move out?"

"I'm not sure."

"When did you move in, sir?"

He affected a laugh. "With all that's been going on, my campaign, my involvement with politics, my businesses, I'm not really certain of the exact date."

"Ballpark guess."

He searched the ceiling again. "Maybe about a month ago."

"And where did your wife go?"

"I don't know. With all due respect, I really can't help you and it's late. As you are aware, I have a guest and I'd like to return to her now. My wife is the furthest thing from my mind tonight." He moved toward the front door. "I appreciate the notification. It's your job to let someone know but if you don't mind, I'd like you to leave."

She and Chaney stepped toward the now open door. "We may have some additional questions for you, Mr. Owens."

"Pete. Call me Pete. I'm happy to talk to you during regular business hours. Just come by the showroom. What do you drive, Detective? We have some spectacular deals going on right now and I'm sure I could negotiate a generous trade-in."

She felt Chaney squeeze her elbow. "Thank you for your time, Mr. Owens." Emphasis on the mister and surname. "And again, we're sorry for your loss."

"Don't be." The door slammed behind them.

Once inside Steel's car and on the road, Parker sighed. "Well, that was enlightening on several levels. I feel like I need a shower."

"Me too. I definitely need some sleep. It's already tomorrow. Let's grab some shuteye and start later today."

"Ten-four."

Rylee plopped on the couch beside Quigley and rubbed his head. "My editor is making me wait until tomorrow to flesh out the story. I told her I dialed Peter Owens and reached his voicemail but she wants me to talk to him, even if he has no comment. I told her the circumstances of my learning Jane Doe's name and she asked me to reconfirm that too."

Nick handed her a glass of sweet tea and sat beside her.

"In a way, I'm glad. This will be one of the hardest stories I've ever reported. I hope I can keep my voice steady."

His arm wrapped around her shoulder. "You'll be your professional self, I have no doubt. I'm glad you're not going to ambush Steel and Bentley by reporting it without them knowing. I agree you are within your right to do so but you don't want to burn that bridge. A couple hours won't make a difference. I doubt any other reporter knows it's Pearl Owens."

She dropped her head on his shoulder. "I still can't believe it. Pearl Owens is dead. Brutally killed. She took me to buy my prom dress. She was beautiful and now, she's bludgeoned to death and unrecognizable. And where the hell is Tessa?"

He kissed the top of her head. "It's very sad. I understand your concern about your friend. She's on Steel's radar now so they may locate her."

"I hope so." She sipped her tea. "You don't think she had anything to do with this, do you?"

"Anything's possible, honey. She was angry with her mother and the nature of the crime was personal."

"So what? She killed her mother and now she's on the run?"

"It's a theory. Her father certainly has the means to make that happen. It could be why she's ghosting you."

"I just don't believe that."

Nick rubbed her upper arm. "It's after midnight and we're both tired. You ready to go to bed? I'm up at six-fifteen and out the door a half hour after that. You've had an emotional night. Let me hold you tonight. A good night's sleep and things may look different in the morning."

"All right. But tomorrow, nothing will have changed. Pearl Owens will still be dead and Tessa will still be missing."

17

Nick woke her with a gentle kiss on the forehead.

"Hey, sleeping beauty, I have to leave. There's fresh coffee in the pot, the garage door opener is on the counter and just in case, I left you the code for the front door. Quigley's already been out and fed so you don't have to worry about him."

She stretched. No sex but spending the night in Nick's bed had been wonderful. She felt rested and relaxed. She dropped her hand over her mouth. "You can't kiss me. I have morning breath."

Nick's laugh was low and sensuous. He drew her hand away and dropped a quick kiss on her lips. "I'll try to call you around lunch. Please be careful today. Don't go anywhere alone and keep an eye on your surroundings. Remember, someone might have eyes on you."

A rush of warmth spread through her. And desire. She laid her hand on his chest. "You sure you can't be a couple minutes late? I wouldn't mind a quickie."

He grinned. "Keep a good thought. I'll see you tonight."

The second she heard the door close she jumped out of bed, smiled at Quigley sleeping in his bed, and hopped in the shower. On the drive to work she reviewed what she had to do. Call Detective Chaney. After last night, she wasn't keen on talking to Parker Bentley yet.

Call Peter Owens. He hadn't returned her message from last night but if she didn't reach him this morning, she'd likely find him prowling the corridors at City Hall. Or at his dealership.

Report Pearl Owens' death. That was going to be the challenge, keeping her voice steady while she used Pearl's name and the word murdered in the same sentence.

Her editor, Tamara, was waiting for her arrival. The researchers had uploaded a flattering picture of Pearl Owens from a charity ball she and Peter Owens attended together three years earlier. They cropped him out and reduced the photo to a headshot. Beneath her chin, a banner read "Murder victim identified."

Rylee shivered but agreed it was a good picture to use. Pearl always looked beautiful, even on her worst days, and Rylee wanted the last picture of her that anyone saw to be favorable.

As she dialed Detective Chaney's number, this was one time she hoped he'd avoid her call. Easier to dump in a phone message that Channel 5 was going on the air at eleven in the morning to tease the story that Jane Doe had been identified and she planned to report her identity on the noon news. No such luck.

"Chaney."

"Good morning, Detective. It's Rylee Lapiz."

"Good morning. My partner owes you an apology. She's not in yet."

"That's fine. I wanted to advise you that I'm going on the air today to report that Jane Doe has been identified as Pearl Owens." She gulped. It was still so hard to fathom. "There were no conditions placed on our conversation last night. Neither you nor Detective Bentley indicated that the exchange of information was off the record and you both know what I do for a living, so there was no expectation of confidentiality." She'd written and rehearsed her spiel before dialing.

Chaney's sigh filled her ear. "That's true but I'd appreciate it if you didn't report it."

"I can't do that, sir. I'm calling to ask for any official comment. On the record."

"Dammit, Rylee, we haven't talked to the assistant district attorney yet. Can't you give us a day?"

"I'm not willing to do that, Detective. Pearl Owens has been dead for two weeks. She deserves better treatment than a toe tag that says Jane Doe. And I don't think one day is going to make any difference to your investigation. If it is, and you give me a good reason, I'll consider delaying the story. But you can't, can you?"

This time he grunted. "No, no I can't."

"Then, do you have a comment for the record?"

"The investigation is ongoing. Anyone who has information about events leading up to Pearl Owens' death is asked to contact us."

"So, you'll confirm for me again that Jane Doe is Pearl Owens?"

"Yes."

"Is there a connection between the murders of Pearl Owens and Dickey Sharpei, who discovered her dead body and then was murdered?"

"I won't comment on that."

"Thank you, Detective. That's what I needed. Have you notified Peter Owens yet?"

"We spoke to Mr. Owens last night."

"And Tessa?"

"We did not speak to his daughter."

"Do you plan to look for her?"

"Are we still on the record?"

"No, we're officially finished with the interview. This is me asking now. I'm really worried about her. She was so angry with her mother for borrowing her car and then, when the car was dragged from the river, the bottom of my stomach dropped out. She—"

"What are you talking about?"

Rylee hesitated. "Before Pearl Owens disappeared, she borrowed Tessa's car. And never returned it. Tessa was fit to be tied. And then Tessa disappeared and the car was found and my insides have been in a knot ever since."

"So, you do know more about this case than you're telling us."

That brought her up short.

"Excuse me?"

"Did you tell anyone that Pearl Owens had borrowed her daughter's car and was unaccounted for?"

She told Nick but she wasn't dragging him into this.

"What a ridiculous question. Who would I tell? And why? My friend's mother borrowed her car and didn't return it. That's hardly headline news. Certainly not something I go running to you about. No one has ever asked me anything about Pearl Owens. You didn't even ask me anything about her last night. Parker was only hell-bent on finding out who I spoke to about Dickey Sharpei, as if discovering that Pearl Owens was Jane Doe was secondary."

The frustration of the last few days surfaced. "When I met Parker for coffee, Pearl Owens wasn't even on your radar. My conversation with her pertained to Dickey Sharpei. That's all she was interested in. And yes, when the car was retrieved from the river, I told the responding police units that I recognized it as Tessa Owens' car and I knew her mother had borrowed it."

Damn, she didn't want to throw Nick under the bus with this. She'd spoken to the supervisor on scene that day as well so, maybe not.

"Pearl Owens wasn't the focus of any investigation that I'm aware of. My friend was angry with her mother. Why would I tell a detective that? Don't turn this on me. I didn't have to contact Parker to begin with. The only reason I did was because I learned things about Dickey Sharpei that confused me and one of those things hit home regarding my friend's whereabouts. I told Parker I was worried about Tessa. And I said I wondered where Pearl was as well. I made a possible connection between what Dickey said he was supposed to do and my friend after I did some digging on my own. It feels like I'm the only one who's doing that."

"All right, take it easy."

"Take it easy? You're trying to make me look like the bad guy." Heads jutted up around the newsroom at her raised voice.

"If that's how you interpreted it, I apologize. It sounds like you know more about this case than you're willing to admit."

"Which case, Detective? I discussed the Sharpei case with Detective Bentley. I never discussed Jane Doe with you or her until I inquired about its status yesterday. I didn't know anything about Jane Doe. I'm sorry now I said anything at all. You'd still be spinning your wheels. I should have called your damn anonymous tipline and left it at that."

"Okay, okay, I see your side of this. Can you enlighten me now?"

If she became part of the story, she couldn't report it.

"No, sir, not right now. This conversation is simply to inform you that I'm identifying Jane Doe on the noon news and seeking comment from you. Do you have anything to add?"

"No, Miss Lapiz, not at this time. But I will be getting in touch with you."

"I don't know why. I'm not the one who killed two people."

Chaney laughed lightly. "Touché."

"I'd appreciate some advance notice if you plan to question me. I'd expect the station's legal counsel to be with me the next time we talk. Not for nothing but I told Parker about the car being dragged from the river. And I filmed the police supervisor at the scene. The station will be happy to provide that news footage for you if you submit a request."

"Can you give me the date of that report?"

She knew it by heart. It was her first date with Nick. But she shuffled papers, drew out a long ummmm and then recited the date.

"Thanks. And Rylee?"

"Yes?"

"We're not adversaries. We've always had a good working relationship. I wouldn't want to see that change."

"Me neither. I wouldn't have called you this morning if I didn't want to keep the lines of communication open and be upfront with you."

"Appreciate that."

"You said you spoke to Peter Owens. How'd he take it? He's my next phone call."

"Off the record?"

"Yes, sir."

"He was unphased. You be careful around him, you hear?"

"You don't have to tell me twice. The man already gives me the heebie jeebies."

She ended the conversation proud of herself for not letting Chaney watch the news and be blindsided by her report. Nick had been right. Again. She smiled just thinking about him and shot him a text. **"Just talked to Chaney. All good."**

He responded with a thumbs-up emoji.

She sent an interoffice note to her editor confirming that she spoke with Detective Chaney and re-confirmed Pearl's identification. She crossed her fingers as she dialed Peter Owens' private cell number. Maybe he wouldn't answer and she could say he couldn't be reached. This was so unlike her. Usually she champed at the bit reaching out to sources and calling contacts. This whole story had her off balance. Talking to Peter Owens was the right thing to do.

"Peter Owens here."

"Good morning, Mr. Owens, it's Rylee Lapiz."

"I'm rather busy right now, Rylee."

"Yes, sir. I'm calling because I know Mrs. Owens was confirmed dead yesterday. We're reporting that today and I didn't want you to see a news report without contacting you."

There was silence on the other end of the phone.

"Mr. Owens?"

"That's considerate of you, hon."

"I also wanted to extend my condolences. Mrs. Owens was good people. Would you like to give me a comment for my report?"

"I'm not comfortable discussing this on the phone. How about we meet? May I buy you a coffee?"

What. The. Fuck was the matter with this man?

"Thank you, Mr. Owens, but my schedule doesn't permit time for that today. I wondered if you wanted to say anything regarding your wife. And have you spoken to Tessa? How's she taking it?"

"I haven't talked to Tessa."

What? Why not? Her mother was dead. All questions that soared through her mind but she didn't pose. Now she was the one who stayed silent.

"What about an early dinner tonight? It might help to have a friend with me."

Friend? She was his daughter's friend, not his.

"Um, thank you but I already have plans. I wanted to call

and express my sympathies and ask if there is anything you want to say officially for the broadcast."

"On the record? No, I have nothing to say. Off the record? Good riddance." The hollowness of his laugh left her speechless.

"All right, Mr. Owens. Well, again, I'm sorry. When you speak to Tessa, please convey my sympathies and ask her to call me. I still haven't been able to reach her."

"I'll do that." The call ended.

One more phone call to make. She dialed the supervisor of the county sanitation department. He'd been avoiding her calls about the circumstances of Dickey's employment. It was unlikely he'd want to discuss a dead employee but she owed it to her audience to find the facts. And she was curious as hell. She left a message seeking comment about R. Sharp.

Well, the hardest part of her day was over. At least until she went on camera. The news anchors teased the upcoming story at eleven and minutes before noon, she stood in front of a green screen. On the TV monitor off to the side, the camera showed her standing in front of the picture of Pearl Owens.

She'd selected a flattering dress to wear today, anticipating the on-camera appearance. Normally, she wore jeans and a decent top with a blazer and was filmed only from the waist up.

The noon news theme played, the anchors announced a breaking news story that viewers would see exclusively on Channel 5 and threw it to her. The hand holding the microphone trembled and her voice cracked.

"That's right, Geoff, Channel 5 news has learned that police have positively identified the woman found dead in the trunk of a car two weeks ago as Pearl Owens, estranged wife of car magnate Peter Owens who ran an unsuccessful campaign for city council last November." Tears blurred her vision.

"Pearl Owens, fifty-seven, was last seen August twentieth by her daughter when Mrs. Owens borrowed her daughter's car, a two-thousand-twenty-three red Mustang. That car was towed from the Allegheny River six days later. No one was inside. Mrs. Owens' body was found on August twenty-first bludgeoned to death in the trunk of a ten-year-old white Chevrolet." The photo behind her on the TV monitor changed to the one she'd snapped that morning. The trunk lid was open and police in uniform and a few wearing jackets emblazoned with the forensics team letters surrounded the vehicle.

"Police have not released any details about that vehicle, which was discovered by twenty-five-year-old Richard Sharpei in the early morning hours in the driveway of his family's suburban home." A high school yearbook photo of Dickey appeared behind her, his hair neatly trimmed, his eyes bright, his smile hopeful. When had he fallen off the rails?

"Sadly, Mr. Sharpei was found dead three days later. He died from a gunshot wound. Police would not comment on whether there is a connection between the two murders.

"Channel 5 news has learned that Mr. Sharpei was a county employee, working under a different name. County officials could not be reached for comment. It doesn't appear his death is linked to his employment but we're digging for more details and will bring them to you as soon as we have the facts. It's a puzzle but we're working to connect all the pieces for you.

"Contacted this morning, Pittsburgh Detective Steel Chaney said both cases remain under investigation. Anyone knowing anything about," she stuttered and swallowed hard, "about the death of Pearl Owens is asked to contact City Detectives." One tear escaped her right eye and rolled down her cheek. Thank goodness this was a distance shot.

"I contacted Peter Owens this morning but he had no comment about his wife's death. We'll be following these investigations closely and bring you the latest updates as soon as we know them. For now, I'm Rylee Lapiz reporting from the Channel 5 newsroom. Back to you, Geoff."

The cameraman signaled the feed had stopped and she dropped her head into her hands and cried. If only Nick was here right now. Her editor waited at her desk and patted her shoulder. "You did fine. I know that was difficult for you but your professionalism shined today."

Her phone pinged and her heart soared to her throat when she read Nick's text. **Well done. Proud of you.**

Through her tears, she smiled. "Thanks, Boss. If you have a minute, I think we need to consult with legal counsel. The detectives will likely want to question me soon. I should fill you in on some things they said about Pearl Owens and information I stumbled on regarding Dickey Sharpei."

AN HOUR LATER, Rylee stormed to the lobby after security called to say the police were at the front door asking for her. She'd told Chaney to give her advance notice if they planned to question her. Her editor agreed that, going forward, she shouldn't talk to them about this story without legal counsel by her side. Chaney and Bentley would have to cool their heels in the waiting area until the attorneys could get here, wasting valuable time they could be using to search for Pearl's killer. And Dickey's, for that matter. After bursting through the doors ready to read them the riot act, she stopped short at the reception desk. Nick waited outside the double glass entry doors in full uniform. Her scowl turned into an ear-to-ear grin.

"Nice surprise. What are you doing here?"

She'd always thought he looked good in his uniform but now, knowing what was under it, he appeared irresistible.

He returned her smile and held up a bag. "Thought you might like a shot of caffeine. I'm sure you need it."

Did she ever. Her heart vaulted. Could he be more thoughtful? "How sweet. Thank you. Aren't you a little out of your jurisdiction? What are you doing on this side of town?"

His head dipped. "Playing hooky so I can't stay. I wanted to see you. You held your head high this morning but I saw the tear and the trembling. I'll wait for you in the parking lot when you get off work. I don't want you to be alone."

She wasn't a crier but today was a day for tear-filled eyes. Her chin quivered. "Okay."

He squeezed her upper arm. "No PDA in uniform. Gotta run. Keep your eyes open."

She strolled back to her desk savoring the aroma of the fresh caramel coffee concoction. And appreciating the man she was falling in love with.

BENTLEY AND CHANEY watched the broadcast on the television in the break room.

Bentley bolted from her chair as if shot out of a cannon. "What the holy hell. What does she mean he was on the county payroll? Where the fuck is that coming from?"

Chaney muted the sound. "The question to ask is why we don't know that. She's been one step ahead of us this whole time. She could have made us look like idiots but she didn't. She reported what she knows without embellishing, I'll give her that." The irony of his statement didn't escape him. The tables had turned and now he was defending Rylee Lapiz to Parker.

"How the hell does she know that?" Bentley pounded her fist on the table. "Dammit. I want to talk to her again."

He'd had enough. "Jesus Christ, you're a little myopic where she's concerned. Is there something between you two? Rylee Lapiz isn't our focus. She's done a better job at connecting the dots between Pearl Owens and Dickey Sharpei but she's not our killer. We're the trained investigators here. If she found out information, we can too. Keep your eyes on the ball. What next, Detective?"

Bentley looked at him wide-eyed and hung her head. He'd never raised his voice to her. That wasn't the way to teach someone. "Sorry. Didn't mean to yell."

"No, you're right. I'm obsessed with Rylee Lapiz when I should be looking elsewhere. The girl is good and currently doing a better job than me. She's convincing people to talk to her who won't cooperate with me. I don't like that feeling."

"So, what are you going to do about it?"

He saw her jaw set, her lungs expand. "Rylee saw a connection between Dickey and Pearl Owens. That's what brought her to me. We can find it too. This is a two-headed monster. We search county records to find Dickey Sharpei and who hired him to do what. Did his parents know he had a job and not tell us? We can loop back to them later. Rylee said he used an alias. His mother's maiden name, maybe? I don't know how she discovered that. Think she's wired in at City Hall?"

"Wouldn't surprise me. She's a familiar face and smart enough to talk up the right people."

Bentley jotted notes on her iPad as she spoke. "So, we talk up the same people. We do a deep dive into Peter Owens. He showed up at Dickey's wake and seemed friendly with the Sharpeis. Was Dickey their connection? Obviously, he had a political motive to kill his wife and protect his reputation. I'd bet he had a financial motive as well. That's easy enough to check. Where was he the night she was killed? I hope not with that piece of fluff he was entertaining in the hot tub. She'd hardly make a good character witness."

Chaney smiled. Parker Bentley was back, focused, determined to find a killer or killers. She continued, "We trace Pearl Owens' last hours, find her friends, figure out her life since separating from the mister. And let's find the daughter. I'll dig up the report on the car towed from the river. Rylee's been unsuccessful in finding her. We locate the daughter and find out what she can tell us about her parents' relationship and her mom. She may have been the last one to talk to her. The daughter should know her friends, possibly her social schedule. Maybe she knows where Pearl was headed when she borrowed her car. And Steel? If we find her, I want to be the one to tell Rylee. I owe her that much."

18

Less than an hour after the noon broadcast, the receptionist rang her desk again. She had a visitor who refused to give her name.

It couldn't be Parker. She'd identify herself as a detective. Rylee didn't recognize the woman.

She was in her twenties, wearing jeans, untied work boots and a skin-tight tank that revealed ample cleavage. She had tattoo sleeves on both arms and several piercings on her face.

"Hi, may I help you?"

"I got someone in the car who wants to talk to you. Follow me."

Rylee followed her to the visitor's parking spot where a beat-up brown car waited, its engine running, the exhaust rumbling. Sour Breath. She approached warily, Nick's words of caution echoing in her head.

Ape Number One sat in the passenger seat, a ball cap drawn low over his sunglass covered eyes. Sour Breath was behind the wheel in the same get up. The woman opened the rear door, its creak screaming for lubricant, and slid inside.

No way was Rylee getting in that car. She crossed her arms over her chest and stood a good two feet away.

Ape Number One flicked his cigarette. "You did good, TV Lady. You didn't find it yet, did you?"

"Find what?"

He smirked. "Listen." One grimy index finger, cracked and dirty, pointed at her. "Dickey had a meeting with his boss. At the construction site. We told him not to go but he never trusted the right people. Said Daddio wouldn't hurt him. He needed a ride and I gave it to him. I hung back just to make sure Dickey wasn't ambushed. Hunkered down, ya know? Behind a couple bulldozers. I couldn't hear but Daddio shouted and slapped Dickey across the face. Smarmy dude, dressed in a three-piece that cost a lot. Shiny shoes walking in all that dirt. He—"

Rylee gasped. "When did this happen? Did you recognize him? Was it Peter Owens?"

"Couldn't see his face. All I'll tell you is that Dickey worked hard that night, digging a hole. I didn't know he could run a backhoe." His chest puffed out. "Kinda made me proud. But I thought he might be digging his own grave so I kept on the down low, you know? When he was done, Daddio handed him something. Looked like a wad of cash. Dickey whooped loud enough for me to hear. He was a sucker for cream. Then he walked away with Daddio. I figured Daddio was giving him a ride back. It was a mighty fine ride, I'll tell you that. I left and we never seen Dickey again."

"What night was that?"

Sour Breath exhaled a cloud of smoke. "Two nights before I told you to meet us. Two of his bitches came in the door when youze was there. We had to shut up. Daddio has eyes everywhere. They been doggin' us."

Ape Number One spit out the window. "We ain't scared, mind you. But we don't want nothin' more to do with this. We gotta go. I got an appointment to keep. Don't tell your cop boyfriend we were here. You never saw us. Daddio ain't a nickname. It stands for something. You got it in the bag."

With that, they rolled past her and exited the parking lot, the ground beneath her feet pulsating to the stereo's volume.

In the bag? What did she have in the bag?

His words puzzled her the rest of the afternoon. Pearl Owens, wife of Peter Owens, was dead. Had Peter Owens conspired with Dickey? Was that why he made an appearance at the funeral home? He had an alibi, the big fundraiser that night. He'd made a point to tell her he was there late.

She called Detectives Chaney and Bentley, but neither answered.

Still no word from Tessa either. Rylee had dialed her cell number every half hour, always receiving a message that the voice mailbox was full before the call disconnected. She swallowed the bile rising in her throat. Surely by now, her father told her what happened to her mother. Tessa couldn't still be angry at Pearl, could she? The poor woman was dead. Viciously murdered. Wouldn't she reach out to her best friend for comfort? Or even to ask questions? Tessa always wanted to know the real story, as she called it, knowing that Rylee sometimes had inside information about a crime. The stuff sources told her off the record.

Her boss approached her in the editing room. "The strain of this story is evident in the dark circles under your eyes, and the timbre of your voice. You sound like a lifetime chain smoker. Go home."

Rylee taped a five o'clock update on both murders, essentially saying there was nothing new to report. The same footage would air at six and eleven. It was unlikely there'd be any more developments today. She should have been on cloud nine because the station's national news affiliates picked up the story. She was being seen in hundreds of homes across the country. Instead, she was drained. And stuck on the unbelievable notion that Peter Owens had something to do with his wife's murder.

She'd texted Nick about leaving early and walked out to the parking lot, phone in hand, dialing Tessa once again. Her heart skipped seeing Nick and Ben waiting in the same visitor's spot Sour Breath had occupied.

Nick opened his arms and she walked into them, her fist bunching up his Polo shirt, her forehead hitting his chest. He didn't speak, just held her close and squeezed. She drew strength from that. They could communicate without words.

Finally, she drew back, wiped her nose with the back of her hand and offered a tremulous smile. "Hi, Ben."

He stepped forward and briefly hugged her. "Hey, Rylee. You did a hell of a job today."

Nick squeezed her waist.

"Thank you. What are you two doing here?"

Nick looked at Ben and then her. "Well, uh, we're here to talk you into packing another bag and coming to stay with me for an extended period of time."

Her eyebrows shot up. "What? No way." Overnight was one thing. An extended stay? They were moving too fast. "Why? Did something happen?"

"How about if we go grab some dinner and discuss it?"

"Discuss what? Let's talk here, now. What's going on, Nick?"

"One of Dickey's posse is in jail."

Ben nodded. "I recognized him from the night we kept an eye on you at the saloon. His name is Wilson Peak. They call him Big Willy. He's the one," Ben pointed to his throat, "with the spider tattoo."

Ape Number One. He was just here. Her voice trembled. "What's that have to do with me? When did this happen? Where? I just spoke—"

Ben interrupted her. "A couple of hours ago. He was

arrested for possession of a large amount of drugs that could put him away for a good twenty-five years. He's looking to make a deal. This conversation is off the record, right?"

Sometimes her job was more of a hindrance than anything else. She harumphed.

"Yes, it's off the record. How big of a bust? I could call the jail tomorrow if you think it's newsworthy. I routinely check in with the public information officer there. That way the details aren't coming from you."

Nick chuckled. "This isn't about a drug bust, honey. Mr. Peak says he has information about a murdered woman. He told one of the officers he wanted to talk to the TV lady."

If he hadn't reached out to grab her arm, she would have dropped to the ground. The cars in the parking lot began to spin like horses on a carousel. She felt lightheaded and her legs gave out. Nick drew her to his side.

"Don't worry, there's little chance that will happen. But it doesn't rule out one of the others in Dickey's gang looking for you. So, we're taking you into protective custody, sort of. You stay with me when you're not at work. When I can't be your bodyguard, Ben will keep an eye on you. Some of the guys you met at the park are also on board."

She squeezed his bicep. "No. No, I don't like that idea. I don't need protection like that. I can't do my job like that."

Nick winked. "We're experts at surveillance. No one will know we're around."

She shook her head. "No. I'll know you're there. This isn't a good idea. And they don't need to look for me. They know how to find me. Big Willy you said? He was here a little while ago." Her index finger pointed to the ground. "In this very spot."

Nick's jaw dropped. "Why? What'd he want?"

It was all such a blur. She pressed her fingers into her forehead and closed her eyes. "Him and Sour Breath. They told me about a meeting Dickey had with his—with someone."

Nick squeezed her elbow.

"Let's get some dinner and discuss this."

Ben nodded his agreement.

"I'm hungry and you look like you could use a drink. I expect Steel will be calling you sometime tonight, as soon as he finds out about Peak. I want to be with you when he does. C'mon, I'll drive. We'll come back for your car."

Nick helped her into his SUV and Ben agreed to follow them. A hundred different questions ran rampant through her head. She spoke to Big Willy, aka Ape Number One, just hours ago. Why did he want to talk to her from jail? What dead woman? Pearl Owens? Did he know Pearl Owens was in the trunk of the car that Dickey discovered? Had Dickey known who it was all along? Did Big Willy know Dickey was supposed to dispose of her body? Dear Lord, if he was bargaining for his freedom, why would he involve her? He could have told her whatever he had to say this afternoon. She couldn't possibly help him.

Her heart raced. What an exclusive news story this could be. Did she dare talk to him? He scared the bejesus out of her. They all did. Her sweat glands overreacted and she reached to hike up the air conditioning.

"You should tell your boss about this," Nick was saying. His voice sounded a million miles away. "Sending you on an assignment alone is not a good idea right now. Who knows if any of that crew is dangerous? Rylee? Are you listening? Are you okay?"

She dropped her head between her knees. She couldn't breathe. No, she wasn't okay. Nick reached to rub the back of her neck. "Deep breaths, honey. We're almost there."

They drove to a sports bar she'd never frequented. He parked, jumped out the driver's side and ran around to her side. He reached behind her seat, found a bottle of water, and handed it to her. "You're okay. Take a sip of this."

As if on automatic pilot, she drank. Nick rubbed small spheres on her back. "It's okay. Take your time."

"Is she okay?" Ben's feet came into view.

"Yeah, she needs a minute. Let's go inside." He eased her out of the seat, steadying her when she stood. Grabbing her tote, he wrapped his arm around her waist and they walked into a noisy, crowded bar area. Ben led them through swinging doors to a quieter dining side, spoke to the hostess and she escorted them to the farthest corner booth.

He sat facing forward and Nick slid in beside her, his back to the door. He'd told her about this. He never sat with his back to the door. Few cops did. It was instinctive.

She asked Ben, "Nick likes to sit facing the door. Can we switch sides?"

Both men smiled. "I've got your backs," Ben said, "don't worry."

Nick kissed her temple. "It's all good, sweetheart. Do you want a beer or something stronger?"

"I'm not sure I want any alcohol at all. My mind is already spinning." Nick ordered three beers and opened the menu. Food wouldn't stay down, she was certain.

"Tell me what Ape Number, er, this Big Willy person said. Why does he want to talk to me? Like an exclusive interview?"

Ben shrugged. "I don't know firsthand. It was change of shift when I saw him being processed. I didn't make the arrest but I noticed the commotion around him so I hung around for a while. The supervisor was calling the district attorney's office when I left after Peak said he wanted to talk to you and he had information about a murder."

She chugged half her beer, relishing the cold liquid as it doused her dry mouth. "Are you sure he meant me?"

Nick patted her thigh. "If he didn't, then there's nothing to be concerned about is there?" The look on his face didn't reinforce his words.

Ben leaned in toward them. "Keep in mind the guy is desperate. He could be grasping at straws. All the same, I thought Nick should know. But no one else can know this information came from me. We have a confidentiality policy at the jail so I'm fucked if you use my name. Excuse my language."

Rylee nodded. "Don't worry about that. I'm grateful that you're telling me about this."

"Well, you're important to Nick so, by default, you matter."

She blinked twice at that. She mattered to Nick's friends? Before she could ask, he drained his mug and stood. "I'm going to hit the road. Reach out when you need me." He nodded to her and shook Nick's hand as the waitress approached. Nick ordered two steak salads.

Rylee dropped back against the booth and slipped her hand into Nick's. It was like slipping into her comfort zone.

"Tell me about Big Willy, honey. Why'd he come to see you today?"

Her head swayed from side to side. "It's so mind boggling. He told me a story about Dickey Sharpei having a meeting with a man Big Willy called his boss. I suspect it was Peter Owens but he said he didn't see the man's face. Big Willy watched Dickey dig a hole with a backhoe, I think at a construction site in the North Hills. I'm not sure about that. He said it looked like the man paid Dickey for his efforts with a wad of cash. They left the site together. That was the last time he saw Dickey alive."

Nick scrubbed his face with his hand. "Jesus, how are you in the middle of this? Who have you told?"

"No one, except you just now. It's not information I can verify for a follow-up story. I can't do anything with it but keep it on background."

"He's a witness the detectives need to know about, honey. You—"

Tired, hungry, and angry, she snapped. "Well then let them

interrogate him. Shame on them if they don't talk to that whole crew. It's not my job to do their job. I have no legal or moral obligation to tell them anything I learn in the performance of my job. I don't even know if it's true."

Nick pursed his lips. "All right, I'm sorry. I didn't mean to imply you should report it to Steel." He resumed holding her hand.

"I didn't mean to snap." She reached for her phone. "What do you think it all means?"

"It could just be a stall tactic. It could mean he'll tell Steel that you spoke to Dickey, which means they might circle back to you. He could tell Steel the backhoe story. That's quite a bargaining chip. But Steel's objective is not you. It's to find out who killed Pearl Owens and Dickey Sharpei. Who are you calling?"

She sighed as her phone informed her the person she was trying to reach had a full voice mailbox. "I've been dialing Tessa every half hour. I can't leave a message. She's bound to pick up one of these times."

"Let's move to the other side of this booth," Nick said when their food arrived. She hadn't eaten all day. Her stomach growled and she dug in.

"Explain to me how this would work? What if Big Willy insists on talking to me? Will I be allowed to interview him?"

"That's not likely for several reasons. Steel and Parker Bentley would never let you, a news reporter, alone in an interview room with a defendant for any reason. A civilian isn't allowed to interact with a suspect. Even if he goes to jail, which he will for now, you'd have to be approved for visitation, and that would be monitored. If he wants a deal, he makes it with the district attorney. And your station's attorneys should object loud and long to you being permitted to speak to a suspect as a means for the detectives to gain information for their investigation. They can't use you as a source. I doubt Peak wants an audience to talk to you and I don't think he plans to give you an exclusive interview."

"He could have told me whatever he has to say this afternoon."

"Exactly. That's why I think he's just trying to buy time."

"But you think Chaney and Bentley will want to talk to me?"

"It's likely. Whether or not you tell them about today is up to you. They're probably pressing him as we speak to know what he knows and what you have to do with it."

Her voice was sharp. "I don't have anything to do with it."

"I know that. Did he say anything else?"

She shrugged. "Just that it's in the bag."

"In the bag?"

"Yes, I have it in the bag. I don't know what that means."

"Well, his buddies are still out there and they probably know. It's only a matter of time before Steel and Bentley talk to them."

"What if Peak tells them I spoke to Dickey?"

"So what? You told them that."

"What if he tells them what they told me that night, that Dickey knew to expect a car?"

"Then they'll know where you got that information and you won't have betrayed your source. He can't hurt you, honey, unless there's something you haven't told me."

"No, you know it all." She declined a second beer and pushed her empty salad bowl aside. "If he can't hurt me, why isn't it safe at my place?"

Nick grinned. "Because all this is supposition on my part. Until we know what's behind Peak's request, he and his pals remain an unknown. And," he wagged his eyebrows, "I like the idea of having you at home with me and Quigley. Let's go get more of your things."

19

Parker and Steel emptied their pockets and locked their cellphones, credentials, and weapons in the deposit box at the county jail. The sheriff tracked down Chaney shortly after nine o'clock the night before, after a series of misdirected calls to the district attorney's office and police headquarters. He and Chaney decided to let Peak stew overnight in lockup.

Parker was a little miffed that Chaney made the decision without consulting her but his point, that they not rush to the jail immediately simply to placate a thug, made sense. Why inflate Peak's ego?

Mutually they agreed not to clue in Laquisha Moore until they knew what they had. Punks like Wilson Peak often made a lot of noise with little to back it up.

The sheriff was waiting once they passed through security. He shook hands with them. "Good morning. Mr. Peak hasn't said much. Just that he wants to talk to the TV lady and he wants his attorney. He gave us this." He handed Rylee Lapiz's business card sealed in an evidence bag to Chaney, which he passed to her.

"I never heard of the attorney he's asking for," the sheriff said. "We haven't contacted him yet. I figure we'll make the call after you talk to him." Parker reached for the sheet of notepaper Peak had scribbled on. She didn't recognize the name either. Chaney eyed her.

"Let's have a chat with Mr. Peak. We can tell him if he lawyers up, he might not get a deal at all. It's worth the bluff."

The sheriff nodded. "He's in interview room number five. I'll take you."

Big Willy lived up to his name. His muscles had muscles. The sleeves of the orange jail jumpsuit strained to wrap around his biceps. He looked like his best friend was a tattoo artist who used Peak's body as a canvas. Parker wondered if there was any part of him besides his face that wasn't inked.

He sat calmly at the metal table, staring at the observation window. Of course, he couldn't see behind it, but his expression assured her he knew someone could be watching. His face was rugged, in need of a shave, but his eyes were clear and piercing blue.

They introduced themselves without shaking hands and sat opposite him. Chaney had taught her to wait, be patient, sit and observe a suspect without jumping right into questioning him. The trio stayed silent for a good ten minutes. Peak barely blinked. This wasn't his first rodeo. Finally, Parker spoke.

"How are you today, Mr. Peak?"

"Is my attorney here?"

"No sir, not yet."

"You bring the TV lady?"

"No sir. We hoped—"

"Then we have nothing to talk about."

Parker smiled. "I suggest you be a little more cooperative if you want to make a deal, sir. We—"

"I suggest you go fuck yourself, lady."

"If you tell us why you want to talk to Rylee Lapiz, we might consider permitting it."

"Who?"

"Rylee Lapiz, the TV lady."

"Nunya."

"Sir?"

"Nunya business. What I got to say to her is private. It's a good story, though."

She folded her hands in front of her on the table. "Why don't you tell us first? And then you can speak to her."

"Why don't you go do what I told you to do?"

"Why did you have her business card?"

Peak laughed, showing gaps in the back of his mouth where teeth used to be. "She has the hots for me. Wanted me to call her."

"It's to your benefit to play ball with us, Mr. Peak. You're facing a lengthy prison term without a deal that we can facilitate."

Peak reached under the table and juggled his hand. "Play ball with this, lady."

Chaney leaned in. "Don't be a moron. You're what? Twenty-seven, twenty-eight?

Peak's lids drooped over his eyes. "Twenty-eight."

"You're looking at turning seventy behind bars, man. You want us to help you, give us a reason to. A wise-ass attitude isn't a reason. If we walk out of here, no one else is going to listen to you. It's now or never."

Peak leveled a hard stare on Chaney. Another glaring contest, except Peak broke first. He squirmed in his chair and looked at the camera in the top corner of the ceiling. "Is that on? You recordin' me?"

Bentley thought the blinking red light was a clue but she nodded anyway. "It's for your protection as well as ours."

"Who sees it?"

"No one outside of this building."

For whatever reason, Peak found that funny. He threw his head back and laughed. "That ain't protection, lady." After another round of silence, he turned the one hand that was cuffed to the metal ring on the table palm up. "Okay, what?"

She exhaled loudly. "You told the intake officer you have information about a murder. Is that correct?"

He stared at Chaney but responded to her. "Yeah. It's good information too."

"A murdered woman?"

"Un-huh."

"Is this the same woman who was found in your buddy's driveway?"

He re-focused on Bentley and grinned, shaking his head slowly.

Parker straightened in her chair. "Another woman?"

"Un-huh. I can tell you some stuff about the woman in the trunk too. But I ain't talkin' until I sign the papers. I want these charges gone and full immunity for anything I tell you. About anyone. And protection when I get outta here. You get those ready for me and I'll sing like a bird."

Chaney cleared his throat. "It's not up to us. We take what we know to the district attorney and she signs off on it, based on our recommendation." He waved his hand through the air. "We can't go to her without solid information, though. It would help if you could give us a few details. She's not going to sign a blank immunity package."

Laquisha Moore would not be an easy sell but Parker wasn't going to point that out. Peak had locked his lips and resumed glaring. She took a shot.

"Who do you need protection from? Your friends? Will they think you're a snitch?"

He laughed again, louder than if she'd repeated a funny joke. "Right now, I'm safer than any of them."

"Where can we find them? I'd like to talk to them."

He shoved his stubby thumb into his chest. "I'm the one you want to talk to. I tell you what I know, you're gonna cross swords with a powerful man when you go nosin' around. Someone powerful enough to make his wife disappear and pay Dickey back for fucking up. I got more, too." He pointed to Bentley. "That TV lady was asking questions. If she's as smart I as think she is, she'll put it together. That could be good or not so good for her."

He tapped the table with his index finger. "Then there's the other one. TV lady don't know about her. Neither do you. She's the ace up my sleeve. You bring me the papers and I'll give it all to you."

"C'mon, Wilson, we can't catch fish without bait. Give us a name."

"When I see the papers."

It was a stalemate. She blew out a breath. "Okay, we'll be in touch. You need anything while you're in here?" Might as well butter him up.

"How about the TV lady? I need to talk to her again. Make sure she finds it."

They'd stood when the guard entered and started toward the door. Bentley spun around. "Again? When did you talk to her last?"

The guard handcuffed him and directed him out of the room. He didn't answer Bentley's question.

"What in the world does Rylee Lapiz have to do with this? You think I'm obsessed with her but I think she's enmeshed in this. Not criminally but somehow."

Chaney's eyebrows rose and fell. "Could be. Maybe I was wrong. What now, Detective?"

"We leave word for Peak's attorney to contact us whenever he arrives. I find it interesting that both he and Dickey requested attorneys we're unfamiliar with. How can they afford out-of-towners?"

Chaney looked equally as baffled.

"In the meantime," she continued, "Peak isn't going anywhere and while I'm curious why he has Rylee's card, we know where to find her when we want to. I say we head to the courthouse and start our research on Dickey Sharpei and Peter Owens."

Chaney agreed.

HOURS LATER, Parker summarized the divorce documents in Owens vs. Owens in a file on her iPad. Pearl Owens accused her husband of screwing everything except the pet dog. Thank goodness they didn't have one. The car business wasn't as lucrative as Bentley thought. By her calculations, if Pearl Owens received half of the profits, the company would dissolve. She wanted outright ownership of her car, all household items, and all jewelry. Some pieces were described in detail and valued over four-thousand dollars apiece. She also wanted sole possession of the house and a vacation time-share. Wondering if Owens would be homeless if the divorce was granted, she ran a property search and discovered the Mt. Washington condo that Owens owned. When did he move back into the homestead?

Try as they may, they didn't discover anything remotely related to Dickey Sharpei. Rylee remained more knowledgeable than them about that. Tessa Owens was another question mark, but low on Parker's priority list.

Peter Owens had sponsored a political rally the night Pearl Owens was killed. There were numerous photos of him at the event. That didn't rule out a role in his wife's murder. They had nothing tangible, but Parker's instinct was that they were following a strong lead.

Finally, the IT folks contacted her about the street video. She was as giddy as a kid on her birthday as she sat in front of the computer screen and let the technician explain the frames. They were able to follow the mysterious man who dropped off Pearl Owens in Dickey Sharpei's driveway three blocks to the east, where a small corner market stood. The store was closed but a motion detector lit up when the silhouette strolled in the parking lot and slipped into the passenger seat of a red Mustang. The car sped away, the driver unidentifiable.

The last two digits of the license plate were visible for a nanosecond but the tech was able to isolate it and enlarge it. It belonged on the red Mustang dragged from the river. Although the car didn't have a plate on it when it was found, the VIN number linked the plate to Peter Owens' car. The one his daughter drove. The one Pearl Owens borrowed on the last night of her life.

20

Laquisha Moore was in court all day and scheduled time to meet them at five o'clock. Overtime all around.

Bentley and Chaney were sitting outside her office when she rushed in. "Sorry, sorry, court ran late. Come in."

She kicked off her stiletto heels inside the door, walked barefoot to a nearby table and unceremoniously dropped her briefcase on it. She plopped down on a love seat against the wall and unbuttoned the jacket of her two-piece suit. Before their very eyes, she morphed from professional prosecutor to worker bee like them. Bentley smiled. Laquisha was a credit to career women.

"My head is still in that courtroom. Remind me why you're here."

Chaney had already directed her to lead the conversation. "We have a gentleman in county lockup who says he has information about a murdered woman, other than Pearl Owens but also can provide information about her. He wants an immunity deal. He was busted with two kilos of cocaine laced with fentanyl and is trying to save his hide."

"So, we let a drug dealer go to catch a murderer? At first

glance, I'm not comfortable with that. Is his information credible?"

"We don't know. He's not giving up much until he has a deal. The only other demand he's making is to talk to Rylee Lapiz from Channel 5 news."

"Over *my* dead body. Who is he?"

"His name is Wilson Peak. He runs with the crowd that Dickey Sharpei hung with. Look, Laquisha, we're spinning our wheels on his murder as well as Pearl Owens. Peak is a habitual criminal. You give him a one-time-only immunity deal and forget this drug bust, it's only a matter of time before he winds up in lockup again. He's not getting away with anything."

She studied the detectives. "You want to hear what he has to say?"

"We do."

She expelled a breath. "Okay, call the jail. Let's go talk to him. I'll instruct my chief of staff to type up an immunity agreement and send it over. Spell his name again for me."

She wrote it down and buzzed her assistant while she dragged a pair of sneakers from under her desk and grabbed a power bar from the top drawer. "I wasn't thinking about dinner anyway."

After passing through security again, they waited for guards to arrive with Peak. Laquisha and the sheriff positioned themselves behind the two-way glass window where they could see and hear everything. Bentley and Chaney took the same chairs they sat in earlier. Chaney laid a legal pad and pen on the table in front of him. She had her iPad but she kept it closed.

Chaney waved off the guard when he attempted to handcuff Peak to the holding ring. A show of good faith.

Peak eyed them. No silent treatment this time. "I didn't get to finish my dinner. You gonna take care of that?"

Chaney nodded. "We can. What are they serving tonight?"

"Meatloaf and mashed taters. Grayish green beans. Pudding was on the tray too."

Chaney grinned. "Chocolate?"

"Yeah."

"Make our trip worthwhile, Mr. Peak, and you'll eat two desserts tonight. The assistant district attorney is interested in what you have to say."

His massive shoulders lifted. "So where is he?"

"*She* is here waiting for us to tell her what makes you worth immunity."

He bunched his beefy cocktail sized fingers into fists on the table and leaned forward. "You got them papers for me to sign?"

"Doesn't work like that. You don't buy something without seeing the goods first, do you? Neither does she."

Peak blinked once, twice. "What about my attorney?"

Chaney leaned back in his chair, dragging the legal pad with him. "Sorry. You can keep your secrets to yourself for the next twenty-five years. You bring your attorney in, we're done."

Bentley felt her breath hitch. Chaney could ruin it all.

"This happens between me and you," he said. "Or no deal."

Peak's gaze dropped to the tabletop. "What about protection?"

"From whom?"

"That hot shit car guy, Pete Owens."

His words were like a shove to Parker's chest. She fell back against the chair.

Chaney's shoulders squared but his face didn't betray his reaction. "Let's keep this legal. Do you waive your right to have an attorney with you and agree to speak with myself and Detective Bentley now of your own free will?"

"Yeah."

"Okay. Good. We're both going to take notes. What about Peter Owens?"

"He killed his wife. Hired Dickey to get rid of the body. Killed Dickey when he fucked up and called the police."

"Can you prove that?"

His head barely moved when he nodded. "There's proof. Written in Dickey's own words."

"Do you have that proof to show me?"

"No. But I know where it is."

"Where?"

"The TV Lady has it."

Parker's head snapped up from the notes she was taking. What the hell did he just say? "You mean Rylee Lapiz from Channel 5?"

Peak nodded more assertively.

Chaney faked a chuckle. "Explain to me, Mr. Peak, why Miss Lapiz would have this information?"

"Because I gave it to her."

Parker's mouth dropped open. Chaney cleared his throat. "I've spoken with Rylee Lapiz several times since both crimes were committed. Are you saying she's deliberately withholding evidence of a murder from us?"

Peak sneered. "I ain't saying anything of the kind. Just that she has it."

"Has what, exactly?"

His hands formed a square with his thumbnails together, the rest of his fingers upright. "A journal. Or a logbook. I don't know what you call it. It was Dickey's record of everything he did with Owens. The drugs he sold him. The small jobs he did. The money he paid him. Dickey wasn't dumb about everything, you know? The minute Owens offered him a job, Dickey went on the defensive. He smelled a rat."

"The job of killing Pearl Owens?"

"Nah, he didn't do that. Owens did that himself. She was gonna wipe him out. Her and her sniveling daughter."

Parker felt her eyes widen. "Do you mean Tessa Owens?"

Peak's bulky shoulders rose and fell. "Don't know her name. But she's dead, just like her mother. And he's walking around free as fuck, sending messages to us, Dickey's friends, warning us we could be next. Burner phones, I think. Untraceable. That's why I need protection. His web of power extends into city hall and maybe the police department, I don't know."

Ironic that he used that analogy with the giant spider tattooed on his neck. Parker couldn't keep quiet. "City hall? Did he orchestrate Dickey's hiring? What do you know about that?"

Peak's howl startled all of them. "What a fuckin' joke. Dickey got paid for doing nothin'. We all benefited. He was solid. Shared the wealth, you know?"

Parker wondered how Laquisha was reacting. It was the first time she was hearing about Dickey's job. They hadn't briefed her on this part of the saga. "But we couldn't find any record of his employment. What was his job?"

"Ask the TV Lady. She said right on the tube she knew."

"What the hell—"

Chaney raised his hand to silence her.

"You said you have information about a second murder."

"That's right, I do."

Chaney waited, one eyebrow arched.

"It's the daughter. She's in the hole Dickey dug."

21

Rylee was flustered. She was running away to hide from what, she didn't know. It wasn't fear. More like dread. Nick had used the word unknown. It was a dilemma because she normally chased the action and searched for the facts. This was the unspecified. But he'd insisted she not stay at her place alone and she had no other friends she could bunk with. She'd given up on calling Tessa.

Nick followed her to her apartment and watched as she tossed more clothes into a duffel bag on the bed. He stood in the doorway of her bedroom, his hands in his pockets. "I'm trying not to imagine another man in that bed with you."

She grabbed a handful of panties and added them to the pile. "Not too hard to do. There haven't been any."

"Honestly?"

She shoved her hair behind her ears and turned. "Yes. I never made time for anyone and I was ashamed to invite someone into this place. I'm still not sure why I let you pick me up here. If I had a date, I usually met them at the TV station."

He grinned as he walked toward her. "Were there many of

those?" He hands wrapped around her waist and he drew her close.

"What are you doing?"

His eyes closed. "I can't pass up an invitation like that." His mouth zeroed in on hers and his kiss sent tiny electric needles through her body. She was losing herself to this man. She didn't resist when he laid her down and began undressing her.

The unknown couldn't hurt her in Nick's arms. And there was no place else she wanted to be.

Quigley was excited to see her. Coming home to these tail wags might not be so bad. Nick headed to the kitchen to make good his promise to brew her a coffee laced with Kahlua.

He heard her as she unpacked her toiletries in the master bathroom. "Damn."

"What's the matter?" he yelled from the kitchen.

Her face split wide with a grin. "I was a little distracted. I forgot to pack the eye drops I need sometimes at night." After making love with Nick, she was lucky she remembered the clothes. The man was an amazing lover.

"Are you complaining?"

"No, sir."

"Is it prescription or something I can run and buy at the drug store?"

She went to the doorway. "It's not that big a deal. I might have some in my bag. Let me check."

She sat on the edge of the bed and dug into the oversized tote, the keeper of her life. Out came her laptop, a pair of socks, spare toothbrush and toothpaste—she'd remembered to pack those. Her Kindle. She laid it on the nightstand, doubting she'd read in bed like she did when she slept alone.

And a book. A grimy, battered, red notebook held together with a metal spiral spine. About five inches long, four inches wide and maybe a half-inch thick. Like the first diary she'd owned as a thirteen-year-old but without a lock and key. The cardboard cover was dog-eared. The book smelled like weed. What the hell?

She flipped it open to the middle of the lined pages. The handwriting was sloppy, faded in some spots where a pencil had been used instead of a pen. Words jumped off the page. *Daddy-O*

Petey-Boy. Likes the nose candy.

Sanitation department. May first. Ha! Ha! Richard Sharp has a fuckin' job.

Her heart jumped to her throat when she read, *Get rid of a car.*

What was this? Why was it in her bag?

She jumped to her feet. In the bag. Wilson Peak said she had it in the bag. He was the one who searched her tote that night at *The Last Sip Saloon*. He must've dropped it in there.

She opened it to the first page, her hands shaking so fiercely, the words blurred. Printed in large letters like a school child might write were the words DICKEY SHARPEI. ONTREPRENORE. It was dated March first of this year. The writing was smudged, as if he'd run his hand over it immediately after writing it.

Page two detailed his score of a pound of marijuana. He'd jotted down estimates for how much money it might yield. A nickel bag for five dollars. A dime bag. A slice. Like pizza? She'd have to do some research on the marijuana market.

She skipped ahead, scanning for the word Owens. There it was. *Owens setting it up. Gonna take care of me. Like a father. Thought it was funny I called him Daddy O.*

Rylee smacked her forehead. Dickey hadn't talked about Daddio. He'd meant Daddy Owens.

Nick called from the living room. "Did you find some?"

She shut the book like a guilty child and shoved it in her tote. This wasn't something she could show him. Not yet.

She left the bedroom, her hands behind her back.

"What's the matter? You're as pale as a ghost. Do you feel okay?"

"Yeah, I, um...it's just been a roller coaster day." She gathered her hair into a ponytail and let it drop freely to her shoulders.

"Did you find your drops?"

"My what?"

"You said you forgot eye drops. Did you find them in your bag?"

No. She found the identity of a killer in her bag. She nodded wordlessly. Whatever else he said as he stood and walked toward her was lost in the jumbled thoughts filling her head. Peter Owens had something to do with Pearl's death. He'd involved Dickey and now Dickey was dead.

"Honey? What's the matter? You're breathing like you ran a marathon."

"I'm just frazzled. Would you mind if I took a hot shower?"

Nick grinned. "Want some company?"

She touched his cheek. "Not this time, thanks. Give me a rain check?"

He kissed her forehead. "Any time. Make yourself at home."

Under the beating stream, the hot water steaming the shower glass, Rylee stood on shaky legs. She needed to show Detective Chaney what she had. What did she have? Proof of a crime, for certain. What else?

She wanted time to read the entire book. And copy it. These were Dickey's last words.

She stepped out of the shower and peeked into the living room. Nick and Quigley dozed on the couch. Closing the bathroom door, she dialed her boss.

"I can't go into detail right now but contact our attorneys. Have them there first thing in the morning. I have information related to Pearl Owens' murder but I don't want to turn it over to the police without them being there. I'll be in by eight."

Sure, Parker and Chaney needed to know about this book. But it wasn't something they had to know tonight.

22

Two groups of uniformed officers, each armed with a search warrant, swooped into Peter Owens' car dealership and his home at eight o'clock Friday morning in a coordinated raid. Bentley accompanied the group to the business. Chaney went to the house. He loved days like this.

Opening the door barefoot, in a white bathrobe, his hair ruffled, Owens was indignant at the intrusion as the cops pushed past him. "What the hell is this? You have no right."

Chaney slapped a copy of the warrant against Owens' bare chest. "Yes, sir, we do."

Owens blanched looking at the top sheet. Spelled out in the paragraph for probable cause was suspicion of and/or involvement with the murders of Pearl Owens and Richard Sharpei. "This is absurd. I'm calling my attorney."

Chaney smiled. "Do it fast. We're confiscating your cell phone too." In the driveway, a flatbed tow truck backed in.

While phoning his attorney he threatened to sue the city, the county, the police department and each individual man and woman on the search team.

Chaney and Bentley had kept Wilson Peak talking for more than an hour the night before and Laquisha worked until almost midnight drafting the warrants. She roused a magistrate out of bed to have it authorized this morning an hour before the teams received the green light to move.

Based on Peak's information, they confiscated computers, cell phones, sales records, documents from a safe at the dealership, which the manager had to open, and a safe at the Owens' home that Peter Owens refused to open. That had taken three men and a dolly to remove from the bedroom closet. Chaney crossed his fingers that its contents were worth it because the hardwood floor and doorframe were damaged in the process.

In the middle of the search, Rylee Lapiz called. He let it go to voice mail, uncertain what if any her role was in this case. Chaney had been careful to exclude Nick Cooper from the group of officers conducting the searches. Not because he didn't trust his cousin. But, as Bentley reminded him, men often thought with the little head first. Rylee couldn't possibly know what was going on unless there was a mole in the department. If that was the case, he'd expect to see her on the sidewalk, cameraman beside her and phone in hand, ready to report a breaking story. Not calling him on his cell.

They left Peter Owens standing on his doorstep, cursing and waving his fist in the air.

RYLEE RUSHED to the TV station at seven o'clock, promptly went to the ladies' room and threw up her morning coffee. Then she sat in the stall and read Dickey's journal cover to cover. Holy shit. Peter Owens had a plan to have his wife killed and paid Dickey five-thousand-dollars to dispose of the car and the body. What happened to that money? Had Owens reneged on his part of the deal because Dickey called the police instead? Sour Breath and Wilson Peak had implied as much.

Dickey wrote boldly at first that he could do it, as if jotting the words on the page empowered him.

But entries after he discovered the body took a different tone. He was afraid for his life.

Rylee cradled the book in her hands like a valuable antique, carried it to the copy machine and began carefully reproducing the pages. Just because this was evidence in a murder case didn't mean it wasn't a reportable story. The only problem was she couldn't implicate Peter Owens in the crimes until police arrested him. And they couldn't arrest him without this information. For now, it was her Catch-22.

After detailing the events leading up to her discovery of the journal, and surrounded by the TV station's legal eagles, she dialed Detective Chaney. It went to voicemail.

"Detective, this is Rylee Lapiz from Channel 5 news. I believe I have evidence that Peter Owens plotted to kill his wife. I want to turn it over to you. Please return this call."

The lawyers instructed her to call Parker Bentley next. She left the identical message, written on the sheet of paper in front of her.

"What happens now?"

Tamara stepped forward. "I don't want you out of the building today. We're monitoring police activity at Peter Owens' home and dealership. I've dispatched a news crew."

Rylee's heart stopped. "That's my story."

Her editor nodded. "And we'll rely on your reporting it. But not this morning. Work up a tentative broadcast we can use if police make an arrest. We'll keep it in the can until then. Let's give the detectives another half-hour and reach out to them again. These attorneys are getting paid to sit here and scroll through their phones. I don't want to pay them all day."

She glared at Tamara.

"It will be fine, Rylee. Trust me." She did.

"Okay. How about if I try calling Peter Owens. If he comments, we can report that."

"See what he says."

Owens snapped when he answered the phone. "What?"

"Hello, Mr. Owens, it's Rylee Lapiz. I'd like—"

"I don't have time to talk to you this morning."

"Yes sir, I know. Can you tell me why the police are at your house?"

"This is politics, plain and simple. A witch hunt designed to make someone high on the food chain look good while besmirching my reputation. Nothing more."

"Mr. Owens, I have a journal that Dickey Sharpei kept that implicates you in the murder of your wife. Do you—"

"You what?" His voice pierced her ear. "What kind of journal? Why do you have it? Surely, you don't believe a thing that dope addict claims."

"I—"

"After all I've meant to you, Rylee, this is how you treat me? You broadcast one word of that diary or whatever it is and I'll sue your news station and ruin you." He disconnected the call.

Always erring on the side of caution, the attorneys shot down the idea of using his comments with a report about the book. Rylee watched the TV screen from the newsroom, jealous of her colleague who stood in front of the car dealership broadcasting the breaking news report.

"Police knocked on the door of these premises precisely at eight o'clock this morning and have conducted an aggressive search of the building. We've witnessed boxes and computer terminals being carried out as all employees who were here at the time were asked to wait outside." The camera feed switched to seven men and women watching the action and two of them saying on camera they didn't know what this was about. One of them speculated tax fraud, likely ending future employment as a car salesman there.

Rylee scanned the action behind the reporter. Uniforms moved in and out of the doors like a well-choreographed Broadway show. Was Nick there? Back to the reporter.

"No one is commenting officially yet but we'll be here for the duration and bring you the latest live from the scene." He signed off and inwardly, Rylee smiled. Those were her sources she'd developed over a long period of time. Secretly she was glad they weren't talking to anyone else.

From the safety of the bathroom stall again, she dialed Nick's number. Damn, another voicemail. Why was no one picking up her calls? "Please call me as soon as you can. It's urgent."

She busied herself until lunch time researching background on Peter Owens and trying to weave together the facts she knew about the man with the claims in Dickey's journal. She tried calling Tessa twice and resisted hurling her phone against the wall when she didn't answer.

"I'm going stir crazy, Tamara. I'm leaving to run out and grab a burger. I'll get it to go and be back ASAP. I've got to get out of here for a little bit." Agreeing to strict orders to avoid both locations where police activity was ongoing, Rylee drove out of the parking lot, elated to see a police cruiser fall in behind her. The smile on her face drooped when she saw that it wasn't Nick, but a female officer she knew from another zone. It followed her to the fast-food restaurant. Although she planned to go through the drive thru, she parked and walked toward the running patrol car. The officer rolled down the window.

"Sure feels like you're following me, Betty."

She nodded. "I am."

"Why?"

"That I don't know. The assignment is to keep you under surveillance and don't worry about being obvious."

There went her appetite. "No idea?"

She shook her head.

"Do you want something to eat?"

A second negative nod.

"Okay, well, I'm heading back to the station after I get my food. Just so you know."

"Nothing personal, Rylee."

She knew that but it felt personal as hell.

This wasn't the protection Nick had talked about. He promised that would be discreet. No, this was something else.

Back at her desk and because curiosity bested her, she strolled to the back entrance of the building. A marked police car sat outside. The attorneys advised there was nothing they could do since the cars were parked on public streets. They pushed her to contact the detectives. This time Chaney answered.

"It's Rylee Lapiz."

"Where are you?"

"At the TV station, but you know that. You have units watching me."

"Stay there."

She went to the bathroom and vomited her lunch. A second call to Nick went to voicemail. Was he avoiding her? Did he know about this?

In the numerous stories she'd reported about people turning themselves in to police, admitting to crimes or simply dealing with them in an official capacity, she'd never appreciated the bodily fear it invoked. Her core temperature spiked to stroke level, she was sure. Her palms were sweaty. Her deodorant failed her and her bowels rumbled. This was ridiculous, she'd done nothing wrong.

Chaney made a formidable entrance into the conference

room, escorted by the news director for the station. It seemed odd not to see Parker beside him. He glared at Rylee. She'd kill for a glass of water.

The station's primary attorney rose, shook hands, and made introductions. "Detective, our reporter has come into possession of a notebook that purports to have been owned by Richard Sharpei. In it, he details drug deals and other criminal activity. He also presents information about Peter Owens and appears to incriminate him in his wife's death. He also expresses fear for his own life from Peter Owens."

He picked up the book. "In the spirit of cooperation and in the belief that this is evidence related to a crime or crimes, we're turning it over to you at," he checked his watch and recited the date and time.

Chaney slipped gloves on before accepting it. That was futile. At least ten people had handled the thing since she'd removed it from her tote this morning. He slipped it into a paper evidence bag.

"How do you come to have this, Rylee?"

She'd been instructed not to speak, which was a good thing because her throat was parched.

The attorney faked a cough. "Miss Lapiz discovered it in her purse last night. She was unaware that she was in possession of it until then."

Chaney glared at her as he spoke. "That doesn't answer the question."

"She believes she came into possession of the journal during a meeting with friends of Richard Sharpei. It's her speculation that one of his friends slipped it into her bag unbeknownst to her."

Chaney's jaw tightened. "How about you let her speak. I know she can. If she doesn't want to talk here, we can go downtown and discuss this at the police station."

Blood rushing through her veins pounded in her ears.

"We've advised Miss—"

She jumped from her seat. "Wait, wait, wait. I know Detective Chaney and I'm not comfortable treating him like this."

She ignored the news director when he ordered her to sit down. She steadied her shaking hands on the table and looked directly at Chaney. Cops liked eye to eye contact.

"You knew I spoke to a group of Dickey's friends at *The Last Sip Saloon*. I admitted that in our phone conversation when you told me that he'd been killed. When I met with them, they checked to make sure I wasn't recording them and one of them searched my bag. The only thing I can think of is that he dropped the journal in there then. I didn't find it until last night."

"Who?"

"I didn't know his name at the time but I know now he's Wilson Peak."

"That was what, more than a week ago? You expect me to believe you had it all this time and didn't know it?"

"Yes, sir. That tote is a catch-all for me. Sometimes there's a change of clothes in there. If the book was at the bottom of the bag, I wouldn't see it unless I was digging for something. I found it last night because I was emptying it searching for eye drops."

"And where was that."

She swallowed the lump in her throat. "At my boyfriend's house."

Chaney's chest expanded with the breath he inhaled. "Does your boyfriend know about this?"

"No sir, no he doesn't."

A look of relief crossed his face.

"I presume you've read the contents of this book?"

The attorney spoke up. "We have. As a reputable news organization, we understand the weight of this information and the importance of its handling. We are not ready to report on it at this time but we will not be precluded from using it in the future."

Chaney looked like he might strangle the man. "We'll be speaking about this again, Rylee."

The attorney was still pontificating when Chaney turned his back and exited the room.

23

Rylee collapsed into her chair. She was the Wizard of Oz scarecrow and all the straw had just been yanked from her body. The attorney was advising her not to have further conversation with any police outside of their presence.

"How am I supposed to do my job?"

Her editor looked equally surprised. "Is that necessary?"

"That would be my legal advice."

"That's not fair," Rylee protested.

Tamara patted her shoulder. "We'll work all this out tomorrow. I'm giving you the rest of the day off. Go get some rest and try to put this behind you." She shifted her position so the attorney couldn't see her face. "You're too valuable to sideline." Her eyes drilled into Rylee's, telling her to play along. "We'll figure something out, maybe re-assign you. I'll re-evaluate the newsroom roster later and see what pieces can be moved."

She trusted Tamara and right now, getting out of this building was the only thing she wanted. It was claustrophobic. She nodded, thanked the lawyers for their guidance and went to her desk. After retrieving her tote, she walked to her car. No watchdog patrol car outside. Chaney must have dismissed them.

Still no word from Nick. That was fine. She wanted to be alone. She drove to her apartment, once again fighting panic when she realized a brand new black SUV with dealer plates followed her. Parking in her neighborhood was on the street and she circled the block twice looking for a space, the black vehicle cruising slowly behind her like a shadow. She parked half a block away from her apartment and stepped out of the driver's side, the trusted pink pepper spray cylinder in her hand. The SUV crawled alongside her route. The driver's window eased down and Peter Owens stared at her.

Rylee kept her gaze straight ahead and quickened her pace.

"I want the book. Don't fuck with me, girlie." She didn't acknowledge his comment. "It will go better for you if you talk to me."

Was that a threat? Did he really plot his wife's murder? She could run to the fire escape and up the two flights probably before he stopped his car and got out. But Nick had said her door was flimsy and if he kicked it in, she'd be trapped. Besides, why give him the satisfaction of knowing she was afraid of him?

She stopped when she heard the roar of a car without a muffler and the heavy, pounding bass reverberating from it. Rolling down the street was Sour Breath's banged up brown Dodge, cigarette smoke wafting out the window. It slowed then stopped behind the SUV and the music grew louder. The car shuddered from the vibration.

Owens looked in his rearview mirror and stepped on the gas, his tires screeching as he sped away, leaving black marks in the street. Sour Breath's car drifted a little farther and he leaned out the window. She couldn't see who was in the passenger seat. "Get inside. We'll wait."

24

The roar of the Harley brought tears to Rylee's eyes. She ran to the door and halfway down the steps, launching herself into Nick's arms, almost knocking him off his feet. The day had robbed her of any courage she possessed. She clung to him and sobbed.

Nick patiently waited for the meltdown to subside, kissing her temple, squeezing her tight and whispering that it was okay. Finally, her nose snotty, her eyes swollen enough to blur her vision, she stepped back and bit her bottom lip. "I have so much to tell you."

He smiled. "That's what I hear. Can you make it up the steps?"

She led him by the hand up the steps and into her apartment. His eyebrows knitted when he spotted a suitcase by the door. "Are you going someplace?"

Her chin quivered. "Would you mind a temporary roommate for a while? I don't think I'm safe here."

Rylee followed Nick on the motorcycle to his house. She fell to the floor and embraced Quigley, giving in to another round of tears. Nick allowed the breakdown, helped her off the floor when it subsided, and nudged a shot of whiskey into her hands. Over the course of the next two hours, she told him about finding the book, its contents, the meeting with Chaney and the lawyers and finally Sour Breath's rescue.

Nick ran his hands through his hair. "Why didn't you tell me?"

"Plausible deniability." She sat up, proud of herself. "I've covered enough criminal proceedings to know you can't be held accountable for something you don't know about." Finally, she felt better now that everything was off her chest and she was safe on Nick's sofa. "I know enough not to involve you like that. I only briefly looked at it last night anyway."

Nick checked his phone, the second time since they'd arrived home. "Honey, do you trust me?"

"Yes, but that's not why I didn't show you the journal."

"I understand and I appreciate that. You're really very smart. That's not why I'm asking." He raised his phone and turned the screen toward her. "This is Steel texting me. He wants to come here and talk to you. I think you should speak to him but I'll support whatever you want. Your lawyers advised against it. Your editor will probably be pissed. But your boyfriend, who happens to be a cop, thinks you should agree to see him."

"Do you know what he wants?"

"My guess is to hear your side of this story without an attorney speaking for you. He has your best interests at heart. And mine. He made sure I was assigned to the gun range today, where the cell service sucks. Plus, he might not trust me but I understand why. He knows how I feel about you."

Her heart fluttered. Nick's text tone sounded again.

Rylee filled her lungs. "Okay. Tell him to come over."

RYLEE JUMPED UP AS FAST as Quigley when the doorbell rang. Midnight was forty-five minutes away. She stood beside the sofa, her hands folded in front of her, her stomach churning. Chaney exchanged hellos with Nick and squatted to the dog. "Hey pups, how're you doing? You've gotten bigger since the last time I saw you." Rylee drew her bottom lip in between her teeth and tried to relax. He wasn't the enemy that the station's counsel cautioned her about.

"Beer?" Nick asked.

Chaney held up two fingers and walked farther into the living room. He actually smiled at her. "How ya holdin' up, kiddo?"

She shrugged. "It's been a hell of a day, Detective. I'm sorry about this afternoon. In that room with my boss and the attorneys surrounding me, I..."

Chaney waved away her words and accepted the longneck bottle from Nick. "Don't worry about it. Sometimes the suits give you no choice. Remember that when the ADA issues you a subpoena."

Her knees gave out and she dropped onto the couch. "Do you think that will happen?"

Chaney sat in a nearby armchair. "That'd be my bet."

Nick sat beside her and offered her a beer. She set it on the end table and reached for his hand. Chaney leaned forward, elbows balanced on both knees. "Let's talk, Rylee. Just me and you."

She told him everything, beginning with what he knew—that she first saw Dickey Sharpei in his driveway the morning Pearl Owens was discovered. Chaney nearly choked on his beer when she described searching his room and finding the drugs and the fake driver's license under the name Richard Sharp. "That's the name he was hired under at the county."

"Damn," Chaney said. "How'd we miss that? How the heck did *you* find it? And how do I find it?"

"You can't use my information?"

He winked. "I'm just here visiting my cousin. That was the

deal Coop insisted on. Don't worry, I'll figure out something. What else?"

She unloaded everything she'd said and done like a sinner confessing to a priest, even offering up details he already knew, like her coffee talk with Parker. Chaney interrupted her once or twice. "Who's Sour Breath?"

"I don't know his name but I sure was glad to see him this afternoon. I haven't gotten to that part yet."

Finally, she told him about Peter Owens following her earlier in the day and, essentially, warning her. "I can't believe he killed Pearl but, in a way, I can see it. Now that you have that book, I hope you put him away for life."

Chaney drained a second beer. "Don't count on that book. There's no way to prove who wrote it. Dickey has a record and would have signed papers, so there's a possibility we consult with a handwriting expert. But it's a cautious validation. None of his friends are pillars of society. They're all shady. A good defense attorney can accuse any one of them of drafting it to cover their own actions. It's not the smoking gun you want it to be."

Her shoulders sagged.

"There's something else, Rylee, something I hate to tell you. All the media attention today focused on Peter Owens and the search warrants. We also had an evidence response team at a construction site in North Hills."

She sat up. "The one that was suggested as a body drop location?"

"Yes. We had information that directed us to an excavation area and we uncovered another body." His plump fingers entwined in front of him. "I'm sorry, hun. It was your friend, Tessa."

The room went black.

25

After his confession, Bentley confiscated Wilson Peak's cell phone, ordered him not to have contact with anyone, and arranged for him to be housed and guarded in an extended stay motel. He was living high off the hog for the moment.

She was barely living, logging twelve and fourteen-hour days rounding up their witnesses, building their case. She and Chaney decided to divide and conquer and over the next week, she went to work finding the rest of Dickey Sharpei's crew. One by one she interviewed Tiny, better known as Timothy Babbes, Doobie, real name Sanford Accent, and Hector Santiago. Tommy Walker, aka Tommy the Thumb, and Angel Molino had better memories when she met with them a second time. Squirrel continued to elude them.

Bentley was disheartened as she and Chaney met for breakfast Friday morning and compared notes. "They're a motley crew. Only two of them have legitimate jobs. The others have dubious sources of income. As witnesses go, they won't present well."

Chaney shrugged. "It is what it is. What did they give you?"

"All the men corroborate Peak's claims about Owens and Dickey's part in the murder scheme. Dickey told them about his meets with Owens. It was all bravado at first. They all say they tried to discourage him from associating with Peter Owens, which strikes me as ironic. After he found the body, they say he was scared. We've kept Peak under wraps so they don't know where he is. They all expressed concern that he is unaccounted for and dead and fear Peter Owens is picking them off individually for what they know, which, I might add, legally is only hearsay."

"What'd you find out about Mrs. Owens?"

"Friends of Pearl Owens attest to the rocky marriage she survived and the volatile breakup. Pearl was just finding herself, just starting to emerge from under Peter Owens' control, they say, when she disappeared. While some of them wondered why they hadn't heard from her, they admitted their own busy schedules prevented them from making an effort to reach out to Pearl. If you ask me, they're nothing but a bunch of self-centered snobs."

Chaney chuckled, then sobered. "I don't have much on her daughter. Tessa Owens' murder for now is a mystery. You saw the coroner's report, drugged, and suffocated. No video surveillance at the construction site so no idea when or how she arrived. Most of the activity over there was on the south side and we found her on the north side. The primary contractor said that grave could have been dug weeks earlier. He's been extremely cooperative."

"What'd you find from her social media sites?"

"The only thing I learned is that I am out of my element there. These so-called four-hundred-plus friends of hers hardly know her. Some never met her. How can you call someone a friend you don't know?"

Bentley grinned. "That's the way it works. You and I are friends and you and your cousin Nick are friends so he shows up on my page as someone I might know. I send him a friend request. He accepts and bam, we're friends."

"It's too superficial for me. I want to be able to look my friends in the eye and have a beer with them. Not exchange pictures of the outfit I'm wearing today."

"It wouldn't look any different than the outfit you wore yesterday," Bentley teased.

"The tie is different. Obviously, you didn't notice. I've got Rylee Lapiz coming in for an official interview this afternoon. The TV station mouthpieces insist on being present. I'd like you in the room with us."

"I feel bad for her. Have you seen the stories she's reporting? A seven-pound tomato in someone's garden and the opening of a new daycare for special needs kids. I bet she's miserable."

Chaney shook his head. "Have you noticed the station hasn't picked up on most of the police activity? They were a day behind on that murder-suicide and never reported the fatal accident on the turnpike. Those news people better wise up and reassign her back where she belongs. Their ratings can't go any lower."

"Listen to you, championing the fourth estate. Next thing I know, you'll have a Facebook page."

Chaney guffawed. "I'm not pro media. Just Rylee. Let's go easy on her. We know she's not the bad guy. There's gotta be a connection between the murders of the mother and daughter but I'll be damned if I can find it. As near as I can figure, Rylee was the last person to see Tessa Owens alive. Besides her killer. I have to wonder if Tessa was the last one to see her mother alive."

"That's one hell of a family if you think daughter killed mother and father killed daughter."

Chaney shrugged. "I don't know what I think."

. . .

Rylee was nervous and somehow looked smaller flanked by three attorneys. She'd lost weight and Bentley heard grief in her voice. She wanted to invite Rylee to get stinking, roaring drunk with an assurance that Bentley would make sure she got home safe. The girl looked like she needed a good bender. Bentley owed her an apology but this wasn't the right time.

Chaney took the lead for the interview and, although she thought she knew the script, he veered off course when he asked about Dickey's employment with the county. They'd never discussed it.

"You reported on September fourth that Richard Sharpei was employed by the county. How did you learn that information?"

Rylee swallowed hard. "One of his friends told me that he had a job with the city or the county, he wasn't sure which. I searched the personnel records and found he'd been hired under the name R. Sharp."

Bentley opened her iPad. This was new information.

"Why were you searching for that name?"

The attorney interrupted. "The methods our reporters use to gather information takes many forms. Miss—" Chaney held up his hand.

"I'm not trying to learn who Miss Lapiz's source was. I'm asking about the shortened spelling of Richard Sharpei's last name." He returned his gaze to Rylee and nodded.

Bentley couldn't believe her story, that she typed s-h-a-r-p when Peter Owens interrupted her and the computer completed the search. Talk about a freaky break.

"Have you reported a follow-up story with that information? How did you confirm they are the same person?"

"I saw a driver's license with that name in Dickey's bedroom."

Bentley thought she might pass out. What the hell was Rylee doing in Dickey's bedroom? She couldn't possibly have been sleeping with him. Dead or not, he was a low life. And she was dating Steel's cousin.

Dumbfounded, she listened to Chaney move on to another subject. She touched his arm but he eyed her, barely shook his head, and continued asking Rylee to repeat what they already knew. His stare told her to stand down.

Rylee didn't offer any new information after that. She blanched when Chaney gave his usual caution not to leave town.

Unlike Dickey's parents, who at least held a service to feign grief for their son, Peter Owens planned nothing for his ex-wife or his daughter. Rylee was the only one who inquired about it. Their bodies remained at the county morgue for now.

"Where in God's name did the info about Dickey's job come from?" Bentley asked once they were alone in the interview room.

Chaney took a deep breath. "Don't ask, Parker. It's muddied waters. Just trust me on this. We have it on the record now. We can call the Sharpeis and ask to search that room."

"She wasn't sleeping with him, was she?"

"Hell no. She was doing her job. Apparently, a better job than we did."

"But how did you know?"

"As a favor to me, partner, let it go."

The Sharpeis were on another cruise and unavailable for additional interviews. Access to Dickey's bedroom and the fake identification would have to wait.

First thing Monday morning, they reported to Laquisha Moore. She wasn't happy.

"Where's my evidence?" She lectured Bentley and Chaney like school children. "I need hard proof to prosecute this bastard. I have nothing but a group of ne'er-do-wells telling a story they could have concocted while sitting around getting high.

"Meanwhile Owens is getting airtime everywhere I look claiming prosecutorial misconduct. He's accusing this office of being corrupt and criminal in unlawfully searching his business and his home. He's had more than a week of free publicity. The news media is kowtowing to him. I'm surprised we don't know when he passes gas. I bet he wishes there was an election tomorrow. He's sending up a smoke screen so thick, I won't be able to find one juror who isn't tainted. The motherfucker is playing the victim, for Christ's sake."

"We're still investigating," Bentley said. "Something will break."

"I'm not waiting any longer. Go arrest him. Get him in my courtroom. I'll work with what I have."

Bentley left the room with one thought—good luck with that.

26

Parker couldn't believe what she was seeing. Reporters were everywhere. Arresting Peter Owens turned into a pop-up circus. Neither she nor Chaney had realized the media staked out his premises so their arrival at his dealership that afternoon was recorded the minute they stepped out of their cars. Owens acted surprised and offended once in front of the cameras that the uniformed police officers had handcuffed him behind his back.

"This is how they treat a reputable community leader," he responded to the flood of reporters seeking comment. "I've done nothing wrong but they need a scapegoat. I'll probably be charged with kidnapping the Lindbergh baby."

Although the reporters demanded to know the charges, she and Chaney remained silent. Bentley thought that if Rylee Lapiz had been among the squawkers, she might have whispered them to her.

Otto Oscuro, Peter Owens' attorney, jumped on the prosecutorial abuse bandwagon. Oscuro was as much a camera hog as his client, taking every opportunity to argue his case in public.

"If the assistant district attorney had real evidence, she would have presented it in the arrest warrant," he said from the courthouse steps after Owens was arraigned and released on one million dollars bond.

Laquisha had unsuccessfully argued that if he could afford the bond, which he could, Owens could easily leave the country and avoid prosecution.

"This is my client's home, his country that he loves," Oscuro had countered. In her head, Parker heard the *Battle Hymn of the Republic* playing.

Rylee's pulse raced as if she was the one arresting Peter Owens instead of watching it unfold on television. Even with his hands behind his back, he looked smug. Chaney's words still echoed in her ears. Dickey's notebook might not be enough to convict Owens. They needed more. She knew the judicial system well enough to know it would take a few hours to process Owens and for him to post bail, which she didn't doubt he would. His business would easily serve as collateral.

Today would be a slow news day for news stories with all the focus on this arrest. Other criminal activity would pale in comparison. Rylee drove to the Owens' home.

She and Tessa had exchanged keys years ago and she'd driven to her apartment after the interview at the police station and retrieved it from the kitchen drawer. With Peter Owens tied up for a couple hours, she could get a look inside that house.

She let herself in the side door of the garage. Tessa had said her parents never locked the inside door, relying instead on the safety of the locked garage doors and the alarm system. The connecting door opened easily into the laundry room and then the kitchen. She quickly punched in the security code.

It was eerily quiet. Only the hum of the air conditioner and the refrigerator broke the silence. Rylee walked straight to the upstairs bedrooms, choosing to search Tessa's first. After all, she'd been lucky when she searched Dickey's room. Her vision blurred momentarily when she entered the room. Most certainly, her heart stopped. All of Tessa's belongings were gone. The room had been converted into a gym with a treadmill, elliptical machine, hand weights, a weight bar, and a bench. She went to the closet and threw open the door. Empty. She clung to the knob to steady herself. There wasn't a trace left of her best friend.

Tessa's death hadn't been made public yet. Would officials have notified her father anyway?

Tears welled in her eyes and she ran from the room toward the master suite. She'd been in this room often enough to know a flowered duvet covered the bed and contrasting curtains hung at the windows. They were gone. Her eyes darted to the triple dresser searching for Pearl's jewelry caddie, ring holders, the velvet box where she knew Pearl's diamonds lived. She and Tessa had been allowed to rummage through them when they played dress up. Everything had vanished.

The shoes. Pearl Owens loved high heels and had a mesh holder behind the door that held more than two dozen pairs. Rylee had paraded around in them, wishing someday to be as glamorous. The back of the door was bare.

Suddenly the room closed in on her, the house threatened to suffocate her. She rushed down the stairs and into the kitchen, coming to an abrupt stop. The last time she stood in this room, sipping coffee with Peter Owens in his bathrobe, she'd sensed something was off. She couldn't place it then but now it hit her like a snowball in the face. The trinkets that had decorated the kitchen, like the crocheted potholder with the Owens name in the center that hung above the stove, the crossed wooden fork and spoon Pearl had brought back from Mexico and displayed between the cabinets, the corkboard that was always overloaded with notes, reminders, and appointment cards—not here now.

They hadn't been here that morning, before anyone even knew Pearl Owens was dead.

What *was* here, what her mind now vividly registered, was the car tag from Tessa's car, the one designed to track her vehicle wherever it went. It dangled from a magnet on the fridge door.

She dragged her phone from her back pocket, shaking so badly she had to steady her arms on the island to snap pictures. Then she ran to her car.

Falling into the driver's seat, she jumped when her phone rang. Nick. Was he watching her? She looked up and down the road but saw no one.

"Hey hon, where are you?"

"What? Why?"

She stomped on the gas pedal.

Nick paused momentarily before saying, "That's an odd response. What's the matter?"

She exhaled loudly. She'd tell him eventually anyway. Uncontrolled words gushed from her mouth. "I just left Peter Owens' house. Tessa's—"

"You what?"

She ignored his yell. "Her room is cleared out. Everything is gone. And there's not a hint of Pearl either. It's like he wiped away their existence. Tessa's tag was there, Nick, the one she had in her car. She told me it was in her car but then she thought it wasn't working. It never made sense but he must've had it. He must have taken it from Tessa's car before, before..."

She burst into tears.

"Rylee, are you driving? Get off the road. Now!"

She edged the car to the curb and took two deep breaths. "I-I'm okay, I'm f-fine. I'm sorry, I didn't mean to scare you. It's okay, I'm stopped and there's no traffic anywhere."

"Where are you?"

"About two blocks from his house."

"What were you doing there?"

"I don't know, I thought maybe I could find something to prove he did it. It was a stupid idea but I didn't get caught so it's okay. I saw they arrested him and I knew no one would be there."

"You didn't think that neighbors might see you sneaking in and call the police?"

"I didn't sneak. I have a key." Sure, it was to the side entrance but why be that specific? "I'm going back to the TV station now."

"Well brace yourself, honey. Unis are on their way there to serve you a subpoena."

"Oh my God! How do you know that?"

Nick remained silent.

"Is it you? Are you serving me?"

"No. But I'll be waiting for you when your day is over."

27

Seventy days.

That's how long they had before they walked into the courtroom. Parker didn't see how they could do it.

Pennsylvania statute establishes that charges filed in a criminal case be presented to a judge to determine if there is enough evidence to warrant a trial. The charges—two counts of second-degree murder—are revealed publicly in the preliminary hearing, where Laquisha presented the barest bones of her case. She successfully protected Wilson Peak's identity, referring to him as a confidential informant, and alluded to written proof of Owens' involvement in murder.

In a prelim, the DA only has to prove a crime or crimes has been committed and that the accused person committed or was connected to the commission of those crimes. Rarely did a judge dismiss charges and risk alienating law enforcement.

It was thin ice Laquisha skated on but the judge ruled the evidence was enough and held the case for trial.

Oscuro made it clear in the courtroom and to the press that he would pursue Owens' right to a speedy trial.

"My client welcomes the chance to prove his innocence,"

Oscuro said in a television interview on a station that competed with Channel 5. "We want this action to come before Lady Justice as soon as possible. It's Mr. Owens' right under the Constitution to have this matter litigated immediately. I'm prepared to present my defense now, today."

Every time he said that sentence, his finger pointed in the air. "The prosecutor is trying to postpone a trial because she knows my client is innocent. We'll wait the seventy days, as the statute allows. But not one day longer."

In subsequent court filings, Oscuro rebutted two motions Laquisha Moore filed seeking a continuance of the trial date to allow investigators more time to build their case. He presented the perceived violations of his client's rights and the judge, up for re-election this year, caved.

The trial date was set.

A little under three months to uphold second-degree murder charges, legally defined as a crime committed while the defendant is engaged as a principal or an accomplice in the perpetration of a felony.

Seventy days to coordinate their witnesses and prove Peter Owens murdered two people, maybe three.

Poor Tessa's case was as cold as the Monongahela River on a January day.

28

On the first day of jury selection, Laquisha looked stunning in a lavender pencil skirt and matching bolero jacket with a deep purple silk blouse beneath and taupe heels. Females in the jury pool would likely appreciate her taste. Bentley sure did. The men might simply enjoy the view.

This wasn't a beauty contest but Bentley felt decidedly unfeminine in her bulky blazer, designed to conceal her shoulder holster, and straight-legged slacks. Sturdy shoes that she could chase someone in if necessary looked pathetic when compared to Laquisha's three-inch stilettos.

She and Chaney had read the questionnaires each juror completed prior to being summoned into the courtroom. Laquisha hadn't shared her strategy so they didn't know if businessmen or housewives were desirable, if she favored single, married, or divorced jurors and what age range she preferred. Selecting a jury isn't an exact science and the defense would have its own line of attack. A lot factored into choosing twelve jurors and two alternates to decide if a man should spend the rest of his life in prison.

Per Pennsylvania statute, jurors are randomly called from a list that combines voter registration rolls and licensed drivers. Parker always said that meant they could at least read, write, and pass a driver's exam. The questionnaires also told them who was employed, their club affiliations such as the VFW or NRA, what television programs they watched and particularly if they liked crime dramas, what news outlets they followed, and whether or not they or a friend or relative had walked on the wrong side of the law. Who knew if the answers were truthful? She preferred to look a person in the eye and ask them if, by some miracle, they'd missed the overly extensive coverage of Peter Owens' misfortunes.

When the first fifty jurors filed into the courtroom, they were in the dark about the criminal case they could potentially be selected to hear. She studied their faces as they trooped to their assigned seats, most of them taking seats behind the counsel tables. The initial sixteen had been told to fill the juror's box, allowing them their first look at the defendant, Peter Owens.

Owens rivaled Laquisha's fashion sense. He wore a charcoal gray three-piece suit with a vivid white shirt and a Windsor knotted gray and black striped tie. The fluorescent lights in the ceiling shone in his polished black shoes. Likewise, his clear-coated fingernails glowed. A small metal container of breath mints sat beside the legal pad and pen in front of him.

His legal entourage outnumbered Laquisha's team. Laquisha, her assistant, and Chaney sat at the prosecutor's table. In what could be photographed for a fashion magazine cover, Owens sat surrounded by a team of six outfitted by Prada and Dolce & Gabbana.

She noticed that some of the jurors recognized Owens immediately. Their widened eyes and raised eyebrows indicated they knew why they were there. Every media outlet and social blog had bookmarked this day on their calendars and rehashed what they knew of the case yesterday, and in some cases what they speculated.

The judge had reserved the last row of the courtroom for reporters but only a handful were there for jury selection. Bentley shook her head at the empty seats. Rylee Lapiz wouldn't miss this.

Jury selection is a tedious process. Sitting behind Chaney in the first row of the gallery, Parker's back began to ache and her head started to pound. No food or beverages were permitted in the courtroom and her mouth was as dry as a rice cake. As if sensing her discomfort, Oscuro poured clear water into a glass on the counsel table and sipped it.

By lunchtime, both sides had only approved three jurors. There was no way the trial would start today.

RYLEE'S EDITOR could have knocked her over with a feather when she tapped her on the shoulder and said she was back on the crime beat.

"The lawyers will allow it?" The higher octave of the last two words verified her surprise.

"The lawyers don't know squat about ratings. We were riding in third place and threatening to overtake second in the market when you were tuned into the police scanner. Now our numbers are the lowest ever. Chad is a good reporter but he doesn't have the contacts you have, nor the news sense." She turned her gaze to the reporter who'd been covering Rylee's beat, sitting at his desk, mesmerized by his phone.

"Look at him. What news is he finding? He's checking what our competitors are broadcasting. I can't afford to have you shelved. The only caveat is that you stay away from the Owens trial and anyone connected with it. If possible, stay out of the courthouse and if you have to go there, stay off the floor where the courtroom is. We don't even want the appearance of a conflict."

"I get it." She didn't have to say it twice. Rylee didn't want to lay eyes on Peter Owens, the murderous bastard. Innocent until proven guilty was the standard but she knew in her heart he was behind the deaths of her best friend and her friend's mother.

Rylee stood. "There was a suspicious fire last night in the East End. I'll make some calls. Jury selection starts today in the Owens case. Someone should sit through it to get a sense of what the attorneys are looking for."

Her editor walked away groaning, calling Chad's name.

She drove to the site of the fire and found the distraught homeowners sifting through what was left of their two-story frame home. She captured a tearful interview with them, hopeful that good Samaritans would step up and help them. She smiled to herself. This was what she was meant to do.

She'd practically skipped into the courthouse the next day. Two deputies who operated the metal detectors at the front door welcomed her back. Amy stood at the reception desk and applauded. Other office personnel who passed her in the hallway smiled and said it was about time. She was humbled.

She may have promised her boss she'd stay away from the Owens proceedings but that didn't mean she couldn't nose around. By the end of the day yesterday, only seven jurors had been seated. She learned that Owens' extensive advertising for his business, his failed campaign and the frenzy of his recent arrest seeped into most people's homes. Many of them admitted they liked the guy and couldn't objectively hear the case, one of the courtroom deputies whispered to her in the hallway. The district attorney had an uphill climb.

29

Steel Chaney decided he'd never retire. Sitting for hours trying to stay alert while the attorneys grilled average citizens about their habits and beliefs was harder than laying bricks, a job he did as a teen. He knew too many retirees who wasted away sitting in front of their TVs. Sitting wasn't for him. He didn't have hobbies, wasn't interested in learning to golf, and didn't want to turn into an alcoholic drinking at the Elks or Moose every day.

He'd work until the day they carried him out of the building. He arched his back in the padded chair, hoping to crack it as he reviewed the jury list. Since day one, an air of tension in this room was palpable. It drained him.

He'd wanted to smack the arrogant look off Peter Owens' face every time a potential juror was dismissed. It was as if his popularity increased as each person left the room. Finally, after three days, seven women and four men were empaneled to hear about the cases of Pearl Owens and Richard Sharpei.

Every seat in the courtroom was taken when the judge banged his gavel and called the proceedings to order. Dickey's posse filled the last row, their shirts tucked in and their hair combed in a half-hearted attempt to look presentable.

Sated by lunch and settled in their cushy chairs, the jurors turned their eyes to Laquisha Moore when the judge directed her to begin.

She stood, buttoned her suit jacket, and approached the podium. He'd gained a sense of appreciation for women's apparel in the days he'd observed the professional Laquisha, dressed impeccably but not so much that the female jurors would resent her. Attorneys are like actors and now, the stage was hers.

"Good afternoon, ladies and gentlemen. As you know, my name is Laquisha Moore and I'm the assistant district attorney tasked with prosecuting Peter Owens on two counts of second-degree murder. It's been a long few days to get to this point, hasn't it? Whew!" She pushed a nonexistent hair back into place and smiled, telegraphing that she was one of them. Two of the women nodded. Atta girl, Laquisha.

"Let me tell you about Peter Owens." She rested on the banister of the juror's box, and leaned in as if she were about to share a giant secret. "Peter Owens is a chameleon. What you see is not what you get. What you see is a distinguished looking middle-aged man who's made a name for himself professionally and politically. What you get is a man who plotted to kill his wife.

"In the early morning hours of August twenty-first, Pearl Owens, Peter Owens' wife of more than twenty years, was found dead in the trunk of a car. She'd been beaten beyond recognition, her fingertips burned to make identification almost impossible. The state will show you that Peter Owens arranged for her murder and orchestrated a plan to dispose of her body, enlisting the aid of a troubled young man whom he offered to pay five thousand dollars for his services. Five thousand dollars is a boatload of money in my eyes. Isn't it to you?"

Heads nodded. They hung on her every word.

"Imagine what it looked like to a twenty-five-year-old who'd run afoul of the law, whose parents were more interested in cruises and social obligations than their wayward son. Imagine what it looked like to Dickey Sharpei. We can *only* use our imaginations for that because that poor boy is no longer with us. The state will show that when Dickey Sharpei failed to act on the plan Peter Owens devised to dump his dead wife's body," her fist dropped with a thud on the railing, startling the panel, "Mr. Owens had him killed too."

Two of the men scowled in Owens' direction. Chaney was beginning to believe Laquisha could pull this off.

"We'll present several witnesses to you to prove our case," she continued, now strolling back and forth in front of them. "They won't be the caliber of people and character witnesses the defense will bring forth. Our witnesses come from the wrong side of the tracks, some of them with police records. If you saw them on the street, you'd likely cross it to avoid interacting with them. I'll be honest, they scare me. But someone you enlist to bury a body isn't going to have won a good citizenship award. Look past what you see when they sit there," she pointed to the empty witness chair, "forget the tattoos and the dirty hair and listen to what they say. They're going to tell you a tale of murder."

Her hand went into the air, the first two fingers creating a V. "Two murders. And when you hear what they have to say, I'm convinced you'll find the defendant Peter Owens guilty as charged on all counts."

Her back straight, her head high, Laquisha strolled back to the table where Chaney sat. He wanted to high-five her.

OTTO OSCURO STOOD, buttoned his suit jacket, and laid a hand on his client's shoulder. Owens grinned and Chaney's hackles rose.

"Ladies and gentlemen, unlike the assistant district attorney, I don't need to introduce myself or to tell you why we're here. It's already been a lengthy process and you know why we're here. To prove Peter Owens is being falsely accused of horrific crimes. Like Miz Moore, I implore you to listen to the case that she presents and then I invite you to ask questions. Questions like where is the murder weapon? Where are the fingerprints? Where is the forensic evidence that every two-bit cop show you've ever watched reveals? Ask where the eyewitnesses are, the ones who can say without a doubt they saw Peter Owens commit these crimes."

He patted the shoulder and Peter Owens shined his billboard smile on the group. "Ask these questions and you'll find out there are no answers. No proof of any kind that Peter Owens is nothing more than a political target."

The judge sat straighter in his seat. Both sides had been cautioned not to turn this into a campaign or political spectacle. Chaney wouldn't mind seeing the guy get slapped with a contempt of court order.

Oscuro backed off. "Ask yourself, ladies and gentlemen, where is the proof? You'll see clearly, there is none. For that reason, I'm confident you'll find my client innocent of all charges. Thank you."

He sat and the courtroom breathed a collective sigh. The judge banged his gavel.

"Ladies and gentlemen of the jury, as it is now almost four o'clock, we are going to dismiss court for today. We'll resume promptly at nine tomorrow morning with the state's first witness. I caution you not to discuss this case with anyone, don't watch, read, or listen to any media coverage of it, and come here tomorrow morning with a fresh, open mind."

Now to the business of murder.

CHANEY KNEW Laquisha's line up of witnesses. She called the professionals first, beginning with Sergeant Wayne Cubb. He testified that he responded to Dickey's 9-1-1 call and described what he saw when the two of them opened the trunk. He recounted Dickey's denial of any knowledge of the victim or the vehicle, detailed the grid search and chain of evidence regarding removal of both.

Laquisha held up a quart-sized clear evidence bag, marked and tagged. "Can you identify this, Sergeant?"

Cubb responded with confidence. "It's a tin of breath mints I found near the driver's side front tire of the vehicle that the body was in."

Owens likely didn't think before covering the mints in front of him with his right hand and dragging them off the table. His attorney grabbed his arm to stop him. But Chaney saw it. So did the jurors. Ha! Ha! Gotcha.

Owens' attorney had challenged in pre-trial motions the admission of any testimony regarding conversations Dickey Sharpei had with anyone and now, he stood and regurgitated those objections so they would be part of the official court record. Once again, the judge's ruling that the testimony was direct evidence—spoken personally to Cubb—was admissible. Chaney gave him credit for trying. It might have planted a seed of doubt in the juror's minds. So could've the mints.

Laquisha shifted Cubb's testimony to his discovery of Dickey's body and subsequent procedures that followed.

Once Laquisha finished questioning him, Oscuro stood in place at the defense table.

"Mr. Sharpei is unable to testify to the veracity of your testimony, isn't that right Sergeant?"

"That's correct."

Oscuro hooked his thumb in his vest pocket. "So, you could

conceivably say anything you wanted and attribute it to Mr. Sharpei, couldn't you?"

Laquisha was out of her chair like a jack in the box. "Objection. Sergeant Cubb is a sworn officer of the law."

Oscuro shrugged in good-old-boy fashion. "It's a hypothetical question, your honor."

Chaney's opinion, that the judge was spineless, reaffirmed itself.

"I'll allow the question."

Cubb conceded that, hypothetically, he could misstate the facts.

"And we couldn't prove otherwise, could we Sergeant, because no one else was part of this conversation except you and Mr. Sharpei."

"I guess not."

Oscuro sat down and Laquisha stood.

"Sergeant Cubb, are you testifying truthfully here today?"

"Yes, ma'am."

She called the assistant deputy coroner assigned to both cases. Chaney squirmed along with the jurors and spectators at the coroner's detailed, often gruesome description of Pearl Owens' death. Pictures taken the morning her body was discovered passed among the jurors, eliciting reactions of horror and repulsion. Photos and testimony about Dickey's death followed.

Oscuro was smart enough not to linger with the coroner. "Sir, in any of those photos or your investigation of these crimes, did you discover who killed Pearl Owens and Richard Sharpei."

"No."

"Did anything you investigated reveal a clue as to their killers?"

"No."

"So, your testimony is primarily that they both tragically died and how they met their untimely end, is that correct?"

"It is."

With three questions, Oscuro discharged two hours that the coroner spent on the stand.

"The state calls Detective Steel Chaney." Laquisha had prepped him well and this wasn't his first time testifying in court. She tediously walked him through his and Parker's investigation, taking a little too long, in his opinion. The jurors weren't focused on him after the first forty-five minutes and looked around the room, at their feet, their fingernails, and at the onlookers. It was thirty minutes past their lunchtime. The microphone even picked up his growling stomach.

"How did you come to contact the Owens family dentist?"

"We received a tip from a local news reporter." No sense introducing her name yet. That night he met with Rylee at Nick's still tugged on his heart. She'd been shattered by the news about her friend and her inclusion in the whole Dickey mess. He felt sorry for her. Parker still didn't know about that meeting. He felt guilty about that.

"And how did you come by Mr. Sharpei's journal?"

"The same reporter. In the spirit of cooperation, her news station turned it over as evidence."

"Have you been able to authenticate the veracity of that journal?"

"Yes."

Oscuro stood when it was his turn to question him. "Detective Chaney, do you have an eyewitness to either of these murders?"

"No."

"Do you have any weapons? The gun used to shoot Mr. Sharpei or a battering ram or baseball bat or whatever was used to kill Mrs. Owens? Are you in possession of those?"

"No."

"Fingerprints of the killer or killers? Any DNA evidence?"

"No."

Oscuro harrumphed and sat down. The judge dismissed the jury for their overdue lunch. Once their bellies were full, the real show would begin.

30

Chaney grumbled and settled into the rolling chair he was beginning to resent. Courtrooms were like churches, commanding respect for their hallowed halls. Everyone instinctively whispered. This was one of the older courts with ornate carvings in the mahogany wood of the judge's bench and intricately designed rails in the banister separating the gallery from the prosecutor and defense tables and the jury box.

Behind him spectators quietly found seats, most taking the spot they occupied before the break. Each person's body heat added to the room's temperature. The air conditioning here could use an overhaul. The creaking fans swirling above their heads did little to move the air. The jurors filed in looking happier than they had ninety minutes earlier.

Bentley was on a manhunt and would miss today's testimony.

The bailiff called the court to order. "All rise."

Laquisha began to paint a picture of Pearl Owens. Only two of Pearl's friends were brave enough to testify about Pearl and what they knew about the Owens' marriage.

"She was an outsider in her own home," one woman said, shaking her head. "It was always just him and his daughter."

He was controlling, they said. She was afraid of him.

"Did he ever threaten her?"

"Yes, after she asked for a divorce. Pearl had a temper and she swore to ruin him personally and destroy his business," the second friend said through tears.

"How do you know this?"

"That night, she spent the night at my house. She told me everything. She was afraid for her life."

"Why weren't you suspicious when days went by and you didn't hear from her?"

"I thought she went into hiding. I thought she was safe."

Their testimony evoked emotions from the panel. Chaney saw chins quiver and tissue removed from pockets to wipe the corners of eyes. The vibe of the courtroom was thick as Laquisha helped the second friend step off the stand.

"The state calls Rylee Lapiz."

All fourteen of them sat forward and strained to see the rear doors open.

Nick entered the courtroom with Rylee but remained standing against the back wall. He wasn't in uniform so the jury wouldn't know he was a cop and wonder why a LEO escorted her in.

The female jurors smiled as if recognizing an old friend. That was good for their side. The male jurors observed her progress from the rear of the courtroom to the witness box with mixed facial expressions. Chaney couldn't gauge their mindset.

He watched most of her newscasts and knew she could dress for the camera but passing in front of him in a black pants suit with thin red lines and low red heels, she projected an unmistakable professional persona. Usually, he saw her in blue jeans and sneakers. She'd pulled her hair back into a sleek ponytail. The look was clean, almost innocent.

He noticed the slight tremor when Rylee raised her hand and swore to tell the truth.

"How are you today, Miss Lapiz?" Laquisha sounded friendly.

Rylee gulped. "Nervous."

"Why is that?"

A tremulous smile creased her face. "I'm used to asking the questions."

Every juror smiled at that, and he wondered if she and Laquisha had rehearsed it. Laquisha smiled too.

"I've been on the end of some of your questions. May I say turnabout is fair play?" Jesus, Laquisha turned and winked at the jury and their smiles grew wider. This was Academy Award stuff.

She established Rylee's journalism credentials, complimenting her on her career, then turned serous. "Let's begin by talking about Pearl Owens, Rylee. May I call you Rylee?"

Rylee smiled and nodded. She briefly recounted childhood excursions with the woman she considered a second mother. She testified to arguments she'd witnessed between Pearl and Peter Owens as their marriage disintegrated, the most recent being the day Pearl threw Peter out of the house. She guessed it to be about four or five months earlier.

She described what she knew of Pearl's disappearance, careful not to repeat anything that Tessa told her. That *would* be hearsay and inadmissible.

Laquisha moved on to Dickey and Rylee kept the jurors' attentions by talking about her investigative techniques. She detailed how she did her job, making phone calls and following leads and how she ended up behind the yellow police tape at the Sharpei home. She relived her approach to Dickey in the bar, seeking an interview, repeated his words and talked about her subsequent chats with his friends.

Chaney knew she was a gritty reporter but strung together

and presented in the form of "just doing my job," he found himself nodding. She was better than Channel 5 deserved. The jurors saw it too. They appeared intrigued by the inside look into the development of the news stories they watched while chewing their chicken dinners each night.

Unlike his testimony, which bored them, Rylee Lapiz fascinated them. Once Laquisha established that the red journal in her hand was the one Rylee discovered in her tote and she asked Rylee to read some of the pages, all fourteen pairs of eyes and ears were riveted to their witness. Well done, Laquisha.

"Dickey's friends aren't the type of people you socialize with, are they?"

"No, ma'am."

"When you were invited to the midnight meeting at *The Last Sip Saloon*, you didn't go alone, did you?"

"No."

"Why was that?"

"I thought they were an unsavory group and that it wasn't safe for me to meet them on their turf by myself."

"You were afraid of them?"

"Yes."

"Who went with you?"

"A few off-duty police officers that I know." Rylee didn't look to the back of the room where Nick watched her. She turned toward the jury each time she responded. Chaney glanced a peek at Nick but he was laser-focused on his girl. She was doing well.

"Are you still skeptical of that group?"

"No, ma'am."

"Please tell the court what changed your mind about them."

"We're taught not to judge a book by its cover, or in this case, a person by their looks. I was guilty of that."

And then came the second zinger. Rylee told them about Peter Owens following her to her apartment, demanding Dickey's journal, and the rescue by Dickey's homeboys. She was the darling of the courtroom, someone they allowed into their homes every day, and Owens had made the mistake of going after her. As they glared at him, Owens appeared to shrink in his chair.

Oscuro stood and approached the witness stand. Rylee leaned back in her chair as he did and it created a menacing scene, as if Oscuro was the one to be afraid of. He held a photograph in his hand.

"You've known Peter Owens since you were what, five years old?"

"Yes, sir."

"Been in his house, ate at his table, even sat on his lap, isn't that true?" He turned the picture to show a young Rylee giggling in Peter Owens' arms.

From the defense table, Owens beamed. Chaney hated that clownish grin. Rylee was right, he could portray The Joker.

"It is."

"This is you, correct?"

"Yes."

"Peter Owens has always referred to you as his second daughter, has he not?"

She fidgeted and readjusted her position in the seat. Up until now, she'd appeared confident. "He has called me that, yes."

"Isn't it true that you had a falling out with Peter Owens' daughter, your best friend, and that you resent his keeping you away from her?"

"That's not—"

His voice rose. "Isn't it true that you pounded on Mr. Owens' front door early one morning demanding to know where your friend was and when he didn't answer your questions, you stormed into his house, straight into his kitchen ignoring his state of undress and tried to entice him into giving you information?"

Rylee gasped but found her composure. "No, that's not true."

Now she looked frightened. Several of the women leaned forward, frowns on their faces. Chaney wondered what Oscuro was thinking. Attacking Rylee could backfire.

"Weren't you jealous of your friend because of who her father was? Didn't you often express your admiration for the man, say he was desirable and invite him to dinner on more than one occasion?"

Rylee's eyes widened. "No. That's not true."

"And he rebuked you." Rylee's mouth dropped open and Oscuro's hand shot into the air. "I'll rescind that question. We'll get back to your infatuation with Mr. Owens. Miss Lapiz, does it say anywhere in that book that Peter Owens killed his ex-wife?" A tactical move. Change the subject and keep the witness off balance.

"No, sir."

"Did you see Richard Sharpei write in that book?"

"No."

"Then how can you testify under oath that it's his book?"

"His name is written on the first page."

"Let's be frank, anyone could have written his name there. For all we know, you wrote his name on that page."

She'd been coached well, either by Laquisha or Nick. It wasn't a question and she didn't respond. Chaney grinned like a proud father.

"If you spoke to Mr. Sharpei, if he told you that he effed up as you so crudely put it, why didn't he tell you himself about the book? Why not hand it to you then?"

Laquisha objected that Rylee couldn't know Dickey's reasons for doing anything and the judge agreed. Rylee must have charmed him too.

Oscuro read the room and saw what Chaney saw. Every juror glowered at him. He was alienating them. "Your Honor, defense reserves the right to question this witness at a later time."

Chaney made eye contact with her as she stepped off the stand and winked. Rylee's lips remained pursed as she exited the courtroom, Nick right behind.

"The state calls Tommy Walker."

Tommy the Thumb began the parade of witnesses who portrayed Dickey Sharpei as gullible, in over his head in a plan to dispose of a body and frightened of the man behind the scheme. Oscuro blew them all out of the water with two questions.

"Did Mr. Sharpei ever identify that man as Peter Owens?" Dickey had never named Daddy-O.

"Did you see Mr. Owens commit a crime or know for a fact that he did?" None of them had.

The day ended on that note. Rylee shone today on the stand. Chaney doubted Wilson Peak would do the same tomorrow.

31

"The state calls Edwin Ardilla to the stand."

Clutching his elbow, Bentley escorted Squirrel into the courtroom and Laquisha directed him to the witness seat.

Chaney watched Owens whisper to his attorney, tugging on the sleeve of his jacket to get close. His head shook. His resting smug face disappeared. For the first time during the trial, he wrote furiously on the pad in front of him.

Credit for finding Squirrel went solely to Parker who browbeat Wilson Peak into telling her where he was hiding and convinced Squirrel he was safer in custody. He'd left town the minute he heard Dickey was dead. Parker tracked him down in West Virginia using fake identification and hiding in a seedy roadside motel.

She was well beyond needing a mentor, Chaney thought sadly. He was going to miss her.

Parker had tried to clean Squirrel up but, like Peak, he was a walking tattoo advertisement. His fingers were permanently stained yellow from chain smoking, he wore his shoulder-length hair in dreadlocks, and his oversized pants hung halfway down his ass despite the belt he wore.

The judge gaveled Dickey's posse into silence after they yelled his name and raised their fists in the air when he entered. They'd filled the back row since day one.

Laquisha got his criminal history out of the way right off the bat. Might as well let the jury know he was far from an upstanding citizen. Squirrel testified he'd known Dickey through grade school and high school. They dropped out together. "We were bros. You feel me?"

She didn't correct the street slang. "Did you and your Bro ever engage in unlawful activities?"

Squirrel squirmed and tugged on the collar of his hoodie. "I don't wanta say sos I don't incriminate myself, you know?"

Two jurors snickered.

Laquisha regrouped. "Let me ask you this. Do you have personal knowledge of a white Chevy that was stolen from a rental car lot sometime around late July or early August?"

His head bobbed. "Yeah, I know about that."

"Are you aware of that because you stole the car?"

"Um, I don't wanna say."

A few more chuckles.

"Mr. Ardilla, the district attorney has granted you immunity from prosecution for that particular crime in return for your truthful testimony today. You can discuss it without fear of repercussions. Did you steal the car?"

"Yeah."

"Did someone ask you to steal it?"

"Yeah, Dickey. He said a friend needed it and arranged for the gate to be unlocked and the keys on the front tire. I just walked in the place, got in the car and drove away. Dickey handed me a grand when I gave him the keys. Easiest bank I ever made."

Oscuro objected to the hearsay testimony but the judge allowed it.

Laquisha continued. "Did you ever ask Dickey who needed the car or for what purpose?"

"No. I didn't want to know."

"Mr. Ardilla, are you familiar with a scheme to dispose of a body that Dickey Sharpei became entrenched in?"

"Yeah. That dude was bad news and I tole him so."

"What dude is that?"

Squirrel inclined his head to the defense table. "Dat dude right there. Owens."

A low murmur crawled through the room.

"Do you know Mr. Owens personally?"

Squirrel raised his cracked, dirt-caked fingers to his mustache and began to pull on the hairs. "We don't hang, ya know? But I know him. I did him a favor one night."

"What night was that."

"The night he offed his wife."

"Objection!" Oscuro screamed over the chatter that erupted.

"Sustained. Counselor, caution you witness about his words."

Laquisha nodded. "Was that the night of August twenty-first, or more specifically, the early hours of that day?"

"Yeah."

"Did Mr. Owens ask you personally for the favor?"

"No, Dickey did."

"And what did Dickey ask you to do?"

"He said someone would hit me up for a ride and when the dawg called, could I pick him up? Dickey said don't ask him no questions. Said Daddy-O would give me gas money so yeah, I said I would."

"Was Daddy-O how Dickey referred to Peter Owens."

"Yeah."

"Did you know it would be Peter Owens who would call when you agreed to provide a ride?"

"Naw, I was just doing Dickey a solid."

"Did you know why this unknown person needed a ride?"

"Nope."

"And did that call ever come?"

"Yeah, man, I was at my crib with my bit—girl asleep. Dude called around three in the morning, like he got no respect for when people sleep, ya know?"

"Did you pick up the gentleman?"

"Uh huh."

"Where?"

"A couple blocks from Dickey's house, at the hajee market we always got beer at."

"What was he wearing?"

"A ratty old hoodie. I thought he musta been high, ya know?" Squirrel leaned forward, resting his elbows on both knees. "Din't say a word. Just jumped in and said 'Drive.' Breathin' hard like he was running from the poleece. Made me a little jumpy, ya know, 'cause I don't need no hassle from The Man."

"You say he seemed nervous?"

"Hell yeah. His hands shook like I was glad he didn't have a beer 'cause he woulda spilled all over my ride. He had on a hoodie pulled up and low on his face."

"Could you see his face?"

"Well, yeah, I looked 'cause, you know, it was my ride. I didn't want him doin' me wrong."

"It was Peter Owens?"

"Yep. It was him." He looked toward Owens again.

"And did he make good on his word and give you gas money?'

Squirrel chuckled. "That and more."

"Tell me what he said and how much he gave you."

"Said 'you ain't never seen me. Keep ya mouth shut'. Handed me a band."

"That's one thousand dollars, is that correct?"

"Yeah."

"Mr. Ardilla, did you come here willingly to testify?"

"Hell no, that bad ass bit—detective dragged my ass here. I got outta town fast after Dickey was iced."

"And why was that, sir?"

"Sheeit, lady, that dude left his wife in that car in Dickey's driveway. Dickey knew too much. So do I."

Oscuro waited for the grunts and whispers to die down.

"Mr. Ardilla, you're a convicted felon on probation, are you not?"

Laquisha rose. "Asked and answered, your honor."

"Did you see Mr. Owens deposit a vehicle in Mr. Sharpei's driveway?"

"Nah, I was waitin' at the market. But Dickey said it would go down that way."

"Objection to hearsay, Your Honor."

The judge considered it, then asked Squirrel if it was a face-to-face conversation with Dickey. "Yeah, man, he said I should stay ready 'cause he din't know when. But I got a life, ya know, things to do. I ain't gonna just sit on my as—sit around and wait for a tone from someone I don't know. Dickey wasn't happy I said that. Said I better be ready."

To Chaney's surprise, the judge allowed the comments to stand.

Oscuro cleared his throat. "Did you see the car or the body that was left in the driveway?"

"Nope."

"Did you ever see Mr. Owens together with his ex-wife?"

"Never laid eyes on him."

"Did you see him kill Pearl Owens?"

"Nope."

Chaney jotted on the tablet in front of him and slid it into Laquisha's line of sight. *No more ?s. Cut your losses, now.*

She waited once Oscuro said he had no further questions, as if debating whether to re-cross. He was no lawyer but he knew the tide had turned with this witness.

"Thank you, Mr. Ardilla. The state calls Wilson Peak."

Peter Owens stood up so quickly and looked toward the door, it made Chaney dizzy. His attorney yanked him back down into his seat. Owens paled.

Squirrel stopped mid-stride and Dickey's posse jumped up when Peak stepped through the door, two deputies close behind.

"We thought you was dead."

"Where you bin, boy?"

"Holy shit."

"You alive?"

The veins in the judge's forehead popped while he pounded his gavel and tried to rein in the commotion. Peak strode to the witness stand like a wrestler walking into the arena about to annihilate his opponent. He fist-bumped Squirrel when they passed.

Chaney watched the jurors' eyes grow wide. Peak's biceps swelled as his arms swung front to back. His neck muscles bulged when he turned his head, assessing the crowd. His fists clenched when those intense blue eyes settled on Peter Owens. Beads of sweat dotted Owens' forehead.

Laquisha stood about five-foot-seven in those heels but next to Peak, she looked diminutive. His untied mud-caked work boots thudded when he stepped up and into the witness box. The compartment barely contained him. The judge banged for silence.

"Good afternoon, Mr. Peak. Let's get your criminal record out of the way, shall we? Suffice to say you're no altar boy, are you?"

Peak shrugged.

"And let's be honest with the court. You've been granted full immunity for your cooperation in this case, haven't you?"

"Yes." He may have looked like a wild man, but his voice was low and deep. Chaney thought of it as a perfect radio voice. Laquisha ran him through a summary of his crimes.

"Were you friends with Dickey Sharpei?"

"Yes. I met him when we were both in holding for different misdemeanors."

"And you became friends?"

"Yes, pretty close, actually."

"Were you aware he'd become involved in a scheme to dispose of a body?"

"Yes."

"Did you know details about that plan?"

"No, but I told Dickey to write the shit down to protect himself."

"And did he do that?"

"Yeah, he did. Kept a notebook in the glovebox of my truck."

Laquisha held up the red spiral notebook. "Is this it?"

"Yes."

"Did you ever see Dickey writing in this book?"

"Yeah, a couple times."

"Where were you on August twenty-first, Mr. Peak, the day a car with a body was left in the Sharpei's driveway?"

"Sleeping it off, I guess. I'd been picked up for drunk and disorderly."

Chaney noticed he wasn't dropping the -ing from his words like he did when they spoke at the jail. The gangsta speak was gone. Peak had graduated high school and attended business school. Somewhere along the way, he chose the wrong path.

"When did you learn what had happened?"

"The next day, I think."

"And what did you hear?"

"That Dickey didn't go through with it."

Oscuro objected to hearsay testimony and the judge admonished the jury to disregard that statement. That instruction always amused Chaney. Wasn't it like putting toothpaste back in the tube? Once you hear it, you can't unhear it.

"Are you familiar with the news reporter, Rylee Lapiz?"

"I wouldn't say familiar. I know who she is."

"Have you ever spoken to her?"

"Yes."

"Tell us about that."

"Dickey was getting a raw deal, you know? We didn't think the police were doing anything about his murder."

Laquisha interrupted. "Who do you mean by we?"

Peak's bear-like hand made a circle in the air. "Our group. Dickey's friends."

In the back row, the posse grinned and nodded.

Laquisha urged him to continue.

"TV lady talked to him the night it happened. She treated him right. She even paid her respects at his wake. We thought maybe she could do some investigating and give Dickey a fair shot. So, we asked her to meet us. I didn't think she'd show but she did. She's got a set. We told her what we could but Owens had spies on us."

"Objection!"

"Sustained."

It wasn't important and Laquisha moved on. As long as Peak talked about Rylee, every juror was rapt with attention.

"Please tell us what you yourself specifically did."

"I took her bag and searched it. The thing is huge. I dropped Dickey's red book into it."

She held it up. "This red book?"

"Yes."

"Did you read the notebook?"

"Yes."

"Did you ever speak to Miss Lapiz again?"

"Yes, at her TV station. And we kept an eye on her."

"Did you know Peter Owens?"

"I do now."

"Please tell the jurors about your relationship with him."

"Dickey introduced me. Owens wanted drugs and I supplied them."

"What types of drugs?"

"Some weed. Mostly cocaine. Never H."

"Heroin?"

"Yes."

"Was that your only interaction with Peter Owens?"

"No."

"Please elaborate for the jury."

Peak leaned back and rubbed his hands along his massive thighs. "Dickey didn't like to drive. He'd lost his license so I usually hauled him around. I waited in the car when he dealt with Owens but one night, Dickey called me over. Owens said he had an insurance issue with a car and the only way he was going to collect was if the car disappeared. I disposed of it for him. A red mustang. Dumped it in the river. The deal was, the car would be left at a construction site, the gate unlocked, and I should take it in the middle of the night. I'd be told when. Only I'm nobody's patsy. I don't go into something blind. I staked out the place three nights in a row waiting for the drop."

Laquisha held up her hand to stop him. "What did you see?"

"The mustang arrived, followed by a battered car, maybe a Chevy. Someone wearing a hoodie dragged something from the passenger seat. All I could tell, it was bulky and wrapped like a mummy. Whoever was in the second car helped load the thing in the trunk. Then the hoodie guy got into the passenger seat and they drove away."

"And what did you do?"

"I waited maybe two hours before I approached the car. There was an envelope on the passenger seat with two thousand dollars in it. That was the deal for payment. I drove the car out of there and dumped it into the Allegheny River."

"Was there anything else in the passenger seat?"

"It was wet. I couldn't tell for sure because it was dark. This was after midnight. I thought it was blood."

"Objection. The witness is not qualified to determine what the substance was."

The judge agreed.

Laquisha turned over her witness.

Oscuro approached Peak like he did Rylee only Peak didn't cower. Chaney scribbled on the yellow pad for Laquisha, *Brace yourself.*

"Mr. Peak, what exactly do you do for a living?"

"Odd jobs. I get by."

"And you had no qualms about getting rid of a car for someone?"

He shrugged like it was an ordinary task anyone might perform. "It was a paying job."

"How far away were you from all this activity?"

"A good distance."

"Are you certain the second car that arrived was a Chevy? Could it have been a Ford or a Dodge?"

"Yes, it could have been."

"Doesn't your friend drive a Dodge? Maybe it was his car."

"It wasn't."

"Are you sure? You said you were far away. Could you tell the color of the second car?"

"It was light, maybe white."

"Maybe. But you're not sure. Could it have been another color?"

"I guess."

"And this bulk that you saw being removed from the vehicle." He spread his hands wide. "Did you wonder what it was? Did you think for one minute that maybe you shouldn't go near the car and instead, call the police?"

"No."

"You said the seat was wet, that it might have been blood yet you didn't suspect anything and do your duty as a citizen and dial 9-1-1? You could have called anonymously."

Peak leveled an icy stare on him. "I didn't call anyone."

"Did you sleep that night with a clear conscience?"

Laquisha challenged and the judge warned Oscuro.

"This person in the hoodie, did you see his or her face? Do you know who it was?"

"No, I was too far away."

"Can you say definitively that it was Peter Owens? It could have been Dickey Sharpei, no?"

"Dickey was a smaller build."

"Did you see that it was Peter Owens?"

"No."

"Did you see the driver of the other vehicle?"

"No."

"Did you at all question what was going on?"

"No."

"You took the money, though, didn't you?"

"Yes."

"And what did you do with the Mustang?"

"Drove it off a boat launch into the Allegheny."

"Was someone with you to drive you home?"

"No, I took a bus."

Oscuro turned to the jury and Chaney could only imagine the look on his face. "So let me get this straight. In the middle of the night, at a closed construction site, you witness a car being delivered, a person struggling to drag out a bulky item and deposit it in the trunk of another car, and you see what you think might be blood in the front seat of a car you step into but you snap on the radio and casually drive away in that car. You dump it in the river and get on the bus to go home. What kind of man are you that the jury should believe one word of this extraordinary story?"

Laquisha sprang from her chair like it was spring loaded. "Objection."

"Withdrawn, Your Honor, I'm not going to waste my time talking to the likes of someone like this."

Laquisha planted her fists on the table and leaned forward.

"Mr. Peak, is this extraordinary story the truth?"

"Yes."

"Do you believe that Peter Owens killed or had Dickey Sharpei killed?"

"Yes."

"Do you admit that you were aware of some type of suspicious, likely illegal activity involved with this car and what you saw?"

"Yes."

"And do you admit that you are providing these truthful details because my office has promised you won't be prosecuted for aiding and abetting in this criminal activity?"

"Yes."

"The state rests."

32

Chaney always felt uneasy when it came time for the defense to present its side of the story. He fretted whether he'd done enough, or in this case if he and Parker had uncovered adequate evidence for the prosecutor to present a believable case. He second-guessed if she explained it clearly for ordinary people to understand, and if the tap dance Otto Oscuro was about to perform would sway them.

This case weighed so heavy, he barely drank the coffee Parker brought him. She was nervous too. A spotted bandage wrapped her thumb.

It was a new day, the jurors were fresh from their morning breakfast, and their faces telegraphed their eagerness to hear Oscuro counter what Laquisha said. Would Oscuro be bold enough to let Peter Owens take the stand? In her office earlier, Laquisha rubbed her hands together in anticipation of the opportunity to question him. His smug face had returned.

Oscuro began by calling character witnesses to attest to Peter Owens' good name, philanthropic endeavors, and community leadership. He promoted the fundraiser that Owens sponsored on August twenty-first as if it were happening tomorrow and called three witnesses who testified they saw Owens there.

On cross-examination, they all admitted to Laquisha they saw Owens before eleven o'clock but never later. Neither he nor Bentley could locate anyone who could prove Owens was there at midnight or after. Laquisha had asked Chaney that on the stand and these three seemed to corroborate it. What was Oscuro going for?

Oscuro dragged in Elliott the bartender and his cousin to characterize Dickey and his friends' raucous behavior most nights at *The Last Sip Saloon*, making sure each noted that often, Dickey Sharpei was so drunk, his friends carried him out the door.

Owens' accountant provided a numbers-heavy, mind-numbing account of his financial solidity and acted surprised when Laquisha forced him to admit that, had the divorce from Pearl gone through, the picture wouldn't be so rosy for Peter Owens. In fact, he would have been precariously close to bankruptcy.

Oscuro called Wilson Peak's parole officer and Squirrel's probation officer. Both men elaborated on the pair's colorful criminal history. Laquisha had laid it all on the table so it wasn't new information the jury was hearing but Oscuro reiterated the details with dramatic flair.

"Isn't it true," he asked Peak's parole officer, "that the amount of drugs Wilson Peak was caught with would have put him in prison until he was an old man?"

"It carried a maximum twenty-five-year sentence."

"So, we can assume that Mr. Peak would say anything to save his life, tell any story the prosecution asked him to for his freedom, can't we?"

Laquisha exploded with an objection and Oscuro withdrew the question but, like he'd done throughout the trial, the seed was planted.

Oscuro called the owner of the construction site where all this alleged illegal activity about cars took place. The man looked like a deer caught in the headlights. Questioning him was like speaking to a fence post. He didn't know anything about any activity that might have gone on there after hours.

Laquisha didn't bother with a cross-examination.

And then, Oscuro rested his case. Chaney almost fell out of his chair. Behind him, Parker disguised her surprise behind a loud cough. The courtroom buzzed with speculation. The judge freed everyone early for lunch. Peter Owens' fate could be decided this afternoon.

RYLEE BREATHED a sigh of relief when she learned the defense had rested its case and would not be calling her as a witness. She remained convinced Peter Owens wanted to keep her out of the courtroom, which was why his attorney said he'd call her back to the stand. The knot in her stomach uncurled a smidge.

Cameras hadn't been permitted in the courtroom so her only account of what transpired each day came from Chad, who reported it for each news broadcast. She prodded him with questions each time the trial recessed, which seemed to help him organize his notes and appear on camera with solid and complete details.

"If I can't report it myself, I want it reported accurately," she explained to one of her colleagues who wondered why she helped the younger reporter who was taking her job. "What matters is what Channel 5 gives its viewers, not whether Chad or I shine. The ruthless attitude in this newsroom is demoralizing."

After lunch, she sat in the first spectator's row behind Chaney and beside Nick, clinging to his hand. Parker sat on her other side. Dickey's posse occupied the last row. They nodded to her when she glanced back at them.

The binders, file folders, documents and legal pads were cleared from both the prosecution and defense tables. Behind her, a cellophane wrapper crackled and the faint aroma of root beer wafted toward her. Every seat was full, every person quiet. A sneeze and whispered, "bless you" broke the silence.

"All rise."

The jury filed in and the judge instructed them. "This is the portion of the trial where the lawyers present a summation of their cases, ladies and gentlemen. You will not hear new evidence. I like to say it's a wrap up of what you've heard over the past week. The assistant district attorney will go first, and then defense counsel. The assistant district attorney will be permitted a rebuttal statement. Miz Moore, you have the floor."

Laquisha stood and buttoned the bolero jacket to her pants suit. She strode to the podium with a legal pad and adjusted the microphone.

"Ladies and gentlemen, first I want to thank you for your service. Your attentiveness over the last six days has been noticed and appreciated. There's no question that two people are dead." Rylee's heart cried out for Tessa, victim number three. Detective Chaney had assured her that case was being investigated.

"There's no question that Peter Owens knew both victims. One of them was trying to ruin him. The other could have easily done so once his wife disappeared. I don't need to review how they died. Those gruesome pictures will stay with you for a long time. For that, I apologize. But murder is horrifying. The man responsible for those murders is just as ugly beneath the three-piece suits and shiny shoes. And our witnesses told you why."

She wove the story of Pearl's death and Dickey's murder around testimony that her key witnesses had given. She was positive, almost authoritative in her declaration that Peter Owens was responsible.

"And so he killed her. To protect his reputation. To maintain his perceived standing in the community. To rescue a business that would have gone under if the divorce was finalized. He beat her mercilessly and as a final insult, stuffed a ten-dollar bill in her bra as if to say, 'this is all the money you'll ever get from me.

"Are you wondering about the cat litter? One hundred and twenty pounds of it. The only other thing in that car besides Pearl Owens slowly dying. That was for Dickey to disguise the odor of a decomposing body. We've shown you the fake driver's license he had. We've circled the construction site on the map where he was supposed to drive the car, dump her body, and cover it with cat litter. Wilson Peak agreed to get rid of one car. Owens would have probably enlisted him to dispose of the white Chevy. You've met Mr. Peak. For another two thousand dollars, he might have done it. No questions asked."

She wiped her hands as if clapping off chalk dust. "And then Peter Owens' problems would be over. Only he didn't count on Dickey Sharpei having a conscience. He bet wrong when he bet that Dickey would do his bidding. And Dickey paid the price for his betrayal.

"His friends know it. That's why they've come forward in open court exposing their dirty laundry and seedy existences, risking ridicule and judgment from everyone in this room. Dickey did the right thing and they did too."

Rylee believed every word. Her heart pounded as if she were delivering the speech.

"It's time for you to do the right thing," Laquisha said. "Pearl Owens deserves it. Dickey Sharpei deserves it, too. Peter Owens isn't worthy of your sympathy." She pointed at him. "Don't look at the man, look at the chameleon. One minute a businessman, the next, a killer. Can I say definitely that Pearl and Dickey died by Peter Owens' hands? No. If I could, he'd be facing first-degree murder charges.

"Do I believe he's the reason they're dead?" She laid her palm over her heart. "With my whole being. Once you review all the evidence before you, you will too. I'm confident you'll return a guilty verdict on two counts of second-degree murder against Peter Owens. Thank you."

She breathed hard as she returned to the prosecutor's table, laid the pad down and slipped into her seat.

The judge asked if the jury needed a break and they shook their heads. Otto Oscuro stood. Rather than go to the podium, he paced in front of the twelve jurors.

He chuckled, looked down at his feet while shaking his head, then raised his gaze toward them. "Ladies and gentlemen, I almost feel like I should apologize for wasting your time this week."

Laquisha's spine straightened and Chaney casually pressed his hand over her arm.

"I asked you at the beginning of this trial to listen to the state's witnesses and posed the same question I ask you now." His hands spread wide. "What evidence?"

"What did you hear from the thieves and drug addicts the prosecution paraded before you that proved Peter Owens is guilty of anything? Where's the evidence beyond the ramblings of felons? How do you know that one night, while drinking their beers and sharing their weed, they didn't concoct this whole story to save their own hides? Wilson Peak surely has a lot on the line if he doesn't testify correctly."

His hands smacked together. "The next twenty-five years of his life to be exact."

"You are tasked with deciding whether Peter Owens will spend the rest of his life as a free man, an innocent man, or whether he will go to prison. There's a legal term, a standard of proof used in criminal trials, that the judge will explain to you called reasonable doubt. The prosecutor must prove beyond a reasonable doubt that Mr. Owens is guilty of the crimes she's charged him with. If even one little question nags at you," he squinted his eyes and left no room between the thumb and forefinger he held up, "about his guilt, that's reasonable doubt. The burden of proof is supported by a preponderance of the evidence. In other words, there's so much evidence against this man, he couldn't possibly be innocent. So, let's look at the evidence you are presented with to reach your decision. At the risk of repeating myself, what evidence?"

He propped his chin on his hand as he paced. "Let's say you return your verdict, whatever that is, and in a week or so you're chatting with your barber or your lady friend about the jury you just served on and they ask, 'what was the murder weapon?' Or maybe they wonder 'where was Mrs. Owens killed' or Mr. Sharpei for that matter." He demonstrated an exaggerated shrug. "You don't know, do you?

"And your friend or your barber asks, 'what was the evidence?' Well, let's see. Besides some shocking photos and the coroner's report, there's a can of mints that the state didn't prove belonged to anyone. There's a fake driver's license that could have been Wilson Peak's or the boy next door. And you have a worn out, notebook filled with barely legible handwriting that looks like a first grader wrote in. In addition to his drug-addicted friends who said," Oscuro dropped one hand on his hip, "'yeah, da book belonged to Dickey. Ya feel me,' the state introduced a respected news reporter to attempt to authenticate the book. But she doesn't really know whose book it was, does she?"

Nick's hand tightened and the jurors turned their focus on Rylee. "It's an intriguing story the prosecutor tells, one that would make a great movie. But in this who dun it you can't really say, can you? Miz Moore asked you to look at the evidence as you debate Pete Owens' future. I ask you to look for what's not there and return a verdict of not guilty."

Rylee's heart raced. Peter Owens was going to get away with murder. Every juror looked at Laquisha expectantly. How could she dispute what Oscuro said?

Laquisha stood and smiled. She walked to the center of the jury box and laid both hands flat on it. Slowly, her head nodded.

"My esteemed colleague is correct. My witnesses are not college educated. Some are dubiously employed while others apparently don't have jobs yet they have money in their pockets. I bet you didn't like what you saw or how they made you feel. But I couldn't find the kind of witnesses that Mr. Oscuro wants you to hear from. You see, my job was to impeach Satan," she twisted and pointed at Owens. "and when you want to convict the devil, you have to go to hell to get your witnesses."

She spun back around, her voice louder. "Like 'em, don't like 'em, I don't care. They are not the issue in this trial despite Mr. Oscuro's efforts to make you believe that. Pearl Owens is dead. Dickey Sharpei is dead. They told you what they know as fact." Her fist pounded the rail.

"They may be dirty and they may have criminal records but that doesn't mean you discount what they said. They swore to tell the truth and they did. That's what you tell your barber and your friend when you explain how you found Peter Owens guilty of murder."

Laquisha stomped back to her chair. The courtroom fell into stunned silence. Even the judge needed a moment to compose himself. His Adam's apple bobbed. "Ladies and gentlemen, the time has come for you to deliberate."

He issued routine jury instructions and everyone stood while they filed out. Then the room erupted with conversation.

Chaney shook Laquisha's hand. Parker leaned over to do the same. Rylee turned to Nick, "What do you think?"

"I learned a long time ago never to predict what a jury will do. Laquisha was strong in her closing. It's a crap shoot."

"If he's found guilty, what's the penalty?"

"The mandatory sentence for one count of second-degree murder is life in prison with no possibility of parole. He's charged with two counts."

Chaney tapped Nick on the shoulder. "We're going up the street for a pop. You two want to come?" Nick looked at her and when she nodded, accepted the invitation.

When they walked out of the courtroom, Dickey's posse waited in the hallway.

"Hey, TV Lady!"

"I'm fine," she said, touching Nick's bicep. "Give me a minute."

Gone was the trepidation she'd felt the first time she walked up to this crew.

"What happens now?" Sour Breath asked.

"We wait. It could be fast or it could take hours. Don't go too far."

"Where are youze goin'?"

Her thumb went over her shoulder. "Just up the street. The bailiff will call the detectives when the jury returns."

"We'll hang close. Will you take a phone number and let us know if anything shakes out?"

"I will," she said confidently. Her mind flashed back to the day she handed Nick her phone. She handed her phone to Sour Breath. "Punch in your number."

She read the name Steve and smiled. "Thanks for watching out for me."

"Thanks for sticking up for Dickey."

33

The jury deliberated through dinner but didn't want to go home. They told the bailiff they were close to a unanimous decision.

Rylee shoved the cold fries around her plate with a fork. She, Nick, Chaney, and Parker sat in a booth at a barbecue joint a block from the courthouse. Chaney was the only one who cleaned his plate.

Off in the far corner, Dickey's friends gathered around a table, as subdued as the four of them.

At ten minutes after ten, Chaney's and Parker's phones dinged at the same time. The jury was back. They'd reached a decision after six hours.

Rylee stood with the others and nodded to the group in the back. Dickey's crew trooped behind three cops and a news reporter in what she imagined was quite a sight. It seemed everyone had stayed close and within minutes the courtroom was standing room only. Usually light shined through the ten-foot-high windows in the courtroom but it was dark outside and eerie inside.

More deputies were positioned around the room, all

standing still with their hands grasped in front of them. But their eyes never stopped assessing the crowd.

"All rise."

The judge glided in, his black robe floating behind him. He banged his gavel.

"I don't know what this verdict is but I want to instruct everyone in this courtroom that there are to be no outbursts when it is read. My deputies are here to ensure everyone will conduct themselves appropriately." He nodded for the bailiff to admit the jurors.

At the restaurant, Chaney and Parker had talked about how the jurors act after they reach a verdict.

"If they look at Peter Owens, we're done," Chaney had said. "If they can't look at him, it's good for us."

Rylee squinted her eyes to study their entrance. The jury foreman was the first one in, a middle-aged man dressed casually. He pressed an envelope against his chest. Written inside was Peter Owens' future. Some of them looked down at their feet as they took their seats. Others surveyed the room. Did any of them look at Owens? She couldn't tell. Her palms were sweaty. Her stomach wished she hadn't ordered a second large coffee.

"Ladies and gentlemen, have you reached a verdict?" the judge asked. The foreman nodded, handed the envelope to the bailiff who passed it to the judge. He read it without any facial expression. Giving it back to the bailiff, he asked the foreman to read it.

The man stood, his hands shaking so fiercely Rylee wondered how he could read the words on the page.

"In the case of the Commonwealth of Pennsylvania versus Peter Owens, pertaining to the death of Pearl Owens and the charge of second-degree murder, we the jury, upon our oaths, unanimously find the defendant guilty."

Owens leapt from his chair. "That's a lie! You can't possibly believe them!" Oscuro sprang up to grab his arms, the deputies rushed to the defense table and the judge slammed his gavel on the sound block. "Mr. Oscuro, bring your client under control now."

"No!" Owens yelled. "It's not true. You'll regret this."

"Shut up," Oscuro barked. He forced him into the chair.

The jury foreman had dropped into his seat, several shades paler. The judge ordered him to continue. It looked like it was an effort for him to stand. His voice cracked.

"In the case of the Commonwealth of Pennsylvania versus Peter Owens, pertaining to the death of Richard Sharpei and the charge of second-degree murder, we the jury, upon our oaths, unanimously find the defendant guilty."

The back row erupted in howls as Dickey's friends jumped to their feet and high-fived each other. Owens screamed and shoved the table away. He flew out of his seat throwing off the hands that grabbed him. The jurors jumped to their feet, their mouths falling open, their eyes wide. The bailiff and two deputies tried to hustle them out of the courtroom.

Chaney and Parker vaulted up and stepped toward the commotion. Nick stood and maneuvered in front of Rylee.

Owens' arms flailed. He pointed at the few jurors still scurrying out of the room. "You're wrong. Do you hear me?"

A handful of the spectators screamed and fled the courtroom in a panic.

Owens thrashed around trying to free himself from the deputies' grasp. His suit jacket was askew, his hair tousled. Oscuro gave up and backed away, hands up in surrender. Owens whirled in Rylee's direction, pointing.

"You'll be sorry. This isn't over. It's on you."

Squirrel and Peak advanced up the center aisle toward her. Rylee choked back the bile in her throat. Nick eased his weapon from his shoulder holster. Parker moved closer to the fray.

"Get him out of here," Chaney yelled to the deputies. Five of them tried to control Owens, snagging his suit jacket, restraining his arms, grabbing at his neck. Owens fought back like a wild animal. When he attempted to reach one of the deputy's guns, Parker dove into the melee, body slamming the bunch, knocking everyone over and landing on top of Owens. She punched him in the face and pressed his shoulders to the floor.

"Stay down you piece of shit if you know what's good for you."

Owens' head fell to the floor and tears filled his eyes.

34

Rylee couldn't stop shaking. The four of them sat in a corner booth, shots of whiskey in front of them.

It had taken a half-hour to settle the courtroom, secure Owens in heavy restraints and remove him from the room. He never stopped screaming, vowing he'd get his revenge.

"Will he?" Rylee asked.

Chaney shrugged. "I wouldn't worry about it. I suspect he'll establish himself as a kingpin in prison and live out his life as a big fish in a small pond."

"But you still don't know who his accomplice was. There is a second person involved in all this, the one who helped him transfer Pearl's body to the Chevy. He's still out there."

Parker agreed. "You're right, he or she is. But Owens is a braggart and eventually he'll pound his chest in King Kong fashion and tell his tale and some prison snitch looking to shorten his sentence or pad his commissary account will reach out to us."

"How long will that take?"

No one answered her.

"I'm planning a small memorial service for Pearl and Tessa next Friday. I'd like it if you'd both be there."

Chaney and Parker nodded. Thanks to Chaney's connections, the morgue released the bodies to Aunt Betty and Rylee assured her she'd handle the arrangements.

"What about finding who killed Tessa?"

Nick's arm went around her shoulder.

"It's an open murder case," Chaney said. "We won't let it go cold."

Her laugh sounded more like a frog's croak. "You have no leads and no idea where to start. It's already cold." Her heart sat heavy in her chest.

"That's true. But we have an aggressive TV reporter nipping at our heels every day looking for news. I doubt she'll let us forget Tessa Owens."

Despite the tears that filled her eyes, the corners of Rylee's mouth edged upward.

"You can count on that."

Thank you for reading **Shady Justice**.
If you enjoyed it, please leave a review on Amazon, Goodreads or wherever you buy books
It's the nicest gift you can give an author.

OTHER NOVELS
BY RENA KOONTZ

When Push Comes to Shoot
Loving Gia to Death
Locked and Loaded For Justice: Saving Gia
The Devil She Knew
Love's Secret Fire
Off The Grid for Love
Broken Justice, Blind Love
Thief Of The Heart
A contemporary romance—
Crystal Clear Love
A suspenseful novella—
Midnight Deadline
A contemporary romance novella—
We Have Tomorrow

Find all of Rena Koontz's books on Amazon,
Barnes & Noble
or wherever you buy books

Here's a sample of **When Push Comes to Shoot**

CHAPTER 1

Blood was everywhere, pooling on the faded Persian rug, splattered against the peeling wallpaper as if an oscillating fan had spread it, coagulated on the pale blue sofa in a spot sunken by years of weight dropped into it.

Emma stared at the sight, her stomach threatening to return her morning coffee even though the asshole deserved this. For a brief moment, her mind drove her back to happier

times in this room. Christmases. Birthday parties. Summer barbecues when the breeze from the trees bordering the property fluttered the curtains. The memories were hazy snippets recalled from some deep recess in her brain she'd almost lost. How long had it been since she stepped foot in this house? Too many years to count.

The place was eerily quiet. Like when the dead are present. Even the birds outside sensed it and stayed silent.

Her brother slouched in front of the TV. His feet were propped on a pile of newspapers, his tea mug leaving yet another ring on the coffee table. Only the TV wasn't on. And he was dead.

Not much had changed in this room since the days when

she was welcome here except the piles of paper, amount of mail, unread magazines and boxes lining both sides of the hallway had tripled. The passage from the living room to the family room was merely a precarious tunnel between the stacks. She shivered.

From his high school picture perched in the right-hand corner of the mantle, her brother stared back at her under a thin film of dust. His eyes were defiant even back then, some twenty-five years ago. Demeaning. Angry.

The sweet odor of blood stung her nostrils and she gulped. Homicide scenes were not her bag. Her eyes watered from the smell. There were twelve years between them, enough of a gap for him to resent a pesky little sister. Nevertheless, she'd worshipped him as her older brother, not comprehending that his disdain for her spread even then, like a slow-growing cancer. Disdain that would mutate into contempt. An attitude she refused to accept once she was older.

She reached for the picture but stopped her hand in midair. She wouldn't touch him if he stood alive in front of her. Why should she touch him now that he was dead?

"Lieutenant?"

She whirled around, the intrusion of the officer's voice startling her, and shoved her hands in her pockets like a guilty child.

"Ma'am, I'm afraid you can't be here. The sergeant asked me to secure the premises from everyone until forensics arrives. The scene hasn't been processed yet."

"That's all right, Officer..." His name gleamed from the polished nametag. "Petrus. I assure you I haven't touched anything. I just wanted to see..." she cleared her throat, "you're right, of course. I'll leave. Do you know where my sister-in-law is?"

"Ma'am?"

"My sister-in-law. The victim is my brother."

The young patrolman snapped to attention. "My condolences, Lieutenant."

"At ease, Officer Petrus. Thank you but it's not necessary. I'm concerned about his wife. D'you know where she is? Was she here when it happened?"

"I don't know, ma'am. You should speak to Sergeant Taylor. I believe he's on the grounds. I'm only assigned to the perimeter."

With one final glance at the couch, Emma walked to the kitchen door, noting the dirty dishes piled in the sink, the opened cereal box on the table and the puddled butter in the container on the counter. The hinges squealed when she stepped outside and inhaled deeply. The door needed oil. Odd. Her brother usually kept up with the house maintenance. Or at least he used to.

The back door had always served as the main entrance because the driveway that crawled up the hill circled the house to this point before descending again. It seemed natural to stop the car here and go inside.

Sergeant Taylor waved her over. "Lieutenant Hunter? What brings you here? Did the chief send you?"

She'd heard the rumors about Taylor's missteps on his last few cases and some off-duty shenanigans that the department frowned upon. The boss certainly wouldn't assign this homicide

investigation to him, would he?

"Relax, Sergeant. I'm not here in an official capacity. The victim is my brother. As soon as I heard the radio call, I came over."

His shoulders visibly relaxed. "My sympathies, Emma. But you know you can't be involved in this investigation. It's a blatant conflict of interest."

"I understand. Are you handling the case?"

"And it means you can't ask any questions. Not without

getting my ass in a sling and I've had enough of that recently." His thumb jabbed the air in the direction of the navy blue four-door making its way up the drive behind the forensics van.

"Here comes homicide now." She shaded her eyes and recognized the unmarked detectives' vehicle.

"Is my sister-in-law still here?"

"She's in the squad car." He pointed to the opposite end of the house. That's when she noticed the blue tarp on the roof, over the second-floor office if her memory was correct. Did the roof leak? Her brother had always bragged about his ability to fix anything. Too bad he hadn't climbed up there and fallen off. An accidental death would have been so much easier.

"Has anyone talked to her?"

"She hasn't said a word since she dialed 9-1-1. I would advise you not to interfere, Emma. You know how territorial homicide gets."

She smiled as she backed away from him. "I told you, I'm not here officially. I just want to check on her."

A young officer she didn't recognize stood sentry beside the rear passenger door of the running vehicle. "Officer, I'd like a minute with her please." Eyeing her lieutenant's bars, he stepped aside.

She opened the door and was smacked in the face with a blast of frigid air. Mary sat in the backseat shivering, kneading rosary beads between her fingers. Emma jumped back and barked at the patrolman.

"Turn this AC down immediately! What the hell are you trying to do, freeze a confession out of her? Shut it off now! And open the damn windows."

She slipped into the seat next to her sister-in-law and reached for her clasped hands. She might as well have dipped them into an ice bucket.

"Are you all right?"

Mary turned vacant eyes on her. No makeup and hair that begged to be brushed. When she was younger, her long blond hair softly fell to her shoulders. Emma supposed the chemo drugs had robbed it of its body and luster. Her face and clothes were clean. Not a drop of blood. Emma leaned forward to see her tennis-shoe clad feet. Not a speck.

"Don't say anything to anyone. They'll take you to the police station. I'll call a lawyer that I know. He's good. Don't speak to anyone until you talk to him. I'll meet you there."

She squeezed Mary's hands reassuringly. "It'll be fine, you'll see."

The urge to lean over and place a kiss on Mary's cheek surprised her. Mary had married her brother twenty-four or twenty-five ago. She didn't remember the exact year, but she'd already graduated from the Academy and secured a job with the Pittsburgh police. No matter. The two women were never close. How long had it been since they'd spoken?

Her brother was a tyrant and Mary a saint for having endured life with him. She assumed Mary's faith had a lot to do with that. She epitomized the word 'sweet.' She wouldn't say shit if it gagged her. She certainly wouldn't violate the sixth commandment. She wasn't a killer. But how could Emma prove that?

When Push Comes to Shoot

wherever you buy books

www.ingramcontent.com/pod-product-compliance
Lightning Source LLC
LaVergne TN
LVHW011947060526
838201LV00061B/4237